DREAMSCAPE

DREAMS OF THE PAST AND FUTURE END-TIMES VISIONS

HADASSAH COHEN

Dreamscape: Dreams of the Past and Future End-time Visions©
Hadassah Cohen, Copyright © 2019

ISBN-13: 978-0-578-55404-4
Printed in the United States of America.

Editing: Carla M. Dean, U Can Mark My Word
Cover Design: Olivia Pro Design

For reprint permission or other communication, please email the author at: Hadassahcohen44@gmail.com

Acknowledgements

I want to thank the Lord Jesus Christ for showing me the dreams and visions to help warn this generation to get prepared for what's coming on the earth. The Bible is always the source of prophecy.

Thank you to my editor and proofreader, Carla M. Dean of U Can Mark My Word, my book consultant, Teresa Beasley, my cover designer, Olivia Pro Designs, and my family and friends for listening and sticking by me through all this.

Introduction

Greetings! Let me first start by saying I do not claim to be a prophet of any kind, nor have I ever been involved in witchcraft. I do not take drugs. I am a regular woman who is a believer in Jesus. I do not worship any person on this earth, except Jesus Christ. My reason for writing this book is to alert, warn, and share the spiritual experiences I've had throughout my life from the time I was ten years old until I reached adulthood. Having made this disclaimer, I hope anyone who reads this book will do so with a clear mind, so they are able to receive the messages I'm about to share. As I began to tell people about my dreams, many said I needed to write a book about them. I came across a friend of mine, Pastor Henry McMullen, who wrote a book titled *It Hurts but It's Necessary*, and through him, I found who helped him with his book. So, here I am. I'm grateful to God for my friend.

Look at my hands and my feet. It is I myself! Touch me and see; a ghost does not have flesh and bones, as you see I have.
Luke 24:39 NIV

This bible verse from the chapter of Luke mentions ghosts —or spirits, depending on the translation. The spirits I have seen were never the demonic type. You know the kind I'm referring to - the ones you see in the movies that are bloody and have skin falling off their faces. No, the spirits I've seen were silhouettes, and some were even fully clothed.

I know some people will be skeptical of what they read in this book, and if I hadn't experienced these things for myself, I probably would be skeptical, too. None of these dreams are made up, though. These are dreams and visions that I have actually had throughout my life. For those who can relate to having dreams, I hope by sharing my experiences that it encourages you to talk or write about your dreams and visions, as well.

When I was about eight or nine years of age, I used to sit in a chair in our living room and close my eyes. Then, as if hovering from the ceiling above, I would see myself sitting in the chair. That out-of-body experience happened to me twice at different times that year. I didn't understand what was happening, nor did I tell anyone about it occurring until now.

Around the age of fourteen years old, I started feeling empty inside. I didn't understand my purpose in life and no longer wanted to live. But, after going to church one Sunday with some of my friends, I felt God tugging at my heart, and my life changed when I gave my life to Christ. I felt myself growing closer to God, and as I began to study His words, he began speaking to my spirit.

In 1984, I started seeing things in my dreams. One night while lying in bed praying to the Lord, I drifted off to sleep. I found myself in the nation of Israel during biblical times, and I was one of Jesus' disciples. We went to the house of the twelve-year-old girl who died, and I witnessed Jesus raise the girl from the dead. I was amazed. He performed other miracles, but I can't recall them. In my dream, I could see Jesus' clothing and the sash across his chest, but I never saw his face or skin. *Then came one of the rulers of the synagogue, Jairus by name, and seeing him, he fell at his feet* ^{23} *and implored him earnestly, saying, "My little daughter is at the point of death. Come and lay your hands on her, so that she may be made well and live.*

Mark 5:22-23 ESV

While he was still speaking, there came from the ruler's house some who said, "Your daughter is dead. Why trouble the Teacher any further?" ^{36} *But overhearing what they said, Jesus said to the ruler of the synagogue, "Do not fear, only believe."* ^{37} *And he allowed no one to follow him except Peter, James, and John, the brother of James.* ^{38} *They came to the house of the ruler of the synagogue, and Jesus saw a commotion, people weeping and wailing loudly...* ^{41} *Taking her by the hand he said to her, "Talitha cumi," which means, "Little girl, I say to you, arise."* ^{42} *And immediately the girl got up and began walking (for she was twelve years of age), and they were immediately overcome with amazement.*

Mark 5:35-38, 41-42 ESV

Reading the scripture about the twelve-year-old girl and which disciples were there in that very room made me gasp for breath. I thought to myself that I could have been looking through the eyes of one of the disciples – the men who started it all, the ones who God gave the courage and power to spread His words. Not only that, but I was in the presence of the creator of the universe. The thought brought tears to my eyes.

My Grandfather

When I was sixteen years old, we lived in a house on the south side of town. While lying in my bed, I happened to glance at my door and saw a man staring at me. He came from the living room area, looked at me, and smiled. I thought it was my father because he looked like him.

But, when I called out to my dad and asked him if he had come to my bedroom door, he replied, "No. I'm laying down."

My father's bedroom was in the opposite direction of the way where the man came.

"There was a man who stood in my doorway and smiled at me," I told my father. "He looked like you, Dad."

What I saw was an apparition, or the spirit, of a man: his face, lazy eye, mouth, head, everything.

My dad told me it might have been his father. I never met my grandfather because he died when my dad was a young man, and at that time, I hadn't even seen a picture of my grandfather.

When my dad showed me a picture of him, and I saw he had a lazy eye, I screamed, "OH MY GOSH! IT'S HIM! THAT'S THE MAN WHO I SAW!"

I don't know what's going on in the spiritual realm, but God is in control of it all. I don't know why my grandfather came to see me, nor did I feel his spirit was evil. It was strange;

I had never seen a spirit until that day. But now, since I'm older, I know God will not send us people who we can't recognize. When God sends someone to see you, you will have no doubt it was them. That person will look actually like themselves, and you won't have to guess if it is them. You will know in your spirit if it's them or not. If it's an evil presence, you will feel it in your spirit.

Beware, demons can impersonate the dead. So, if you have any doubt, call out loud in the name of Jesus and tell it to be gone. Demons have to obey because of the name of Jesus.

It's important to know that demons can impersonate the dead. People tell me, "I think I saw my relative," and they very well could have. But, listen to your spirit when you do. Your spirit will feel peaceful if they are from God and an eerie feeling if they are not.

Everyone's experience is different. Some people have told me that their loved one came to them in spirit and didn't say anything. Just showed up and left. Come to find out that relative of theirs had just died. I don't understand all that is happening in the spiritual world, but when God is ready to reveal it, He will to those who are willing to listen.

God understands our grief when we lose a close relative. He knows how much it hurts because he lost his stepdad, Joseph, and his cousin, John the Baptist. I'm sure He lost other friends and family while on Earth. So, you see, he is a God who knows all that we go through in this life.

The name of the Lord is a strong tower: the righteous run into it, and is safe.

Proverbs 18:10 KJV

For God is not the author of confusion, but of peace, as in all churches of the saints.

1 Corinthians 14:33 KJV

In order that Satan might not outwit us. For we are not unaware of his schemes.

2 Corinthians 2:11 NIV

The Shaking

My family and I moved from the West to the Midwest in the '70s. My mother and father bought a house on the east side of town. It was an older home, only one level. Around 1980, when I was ten years old, I started sensing something in the house. Sometimes when in my room alone, it would feel like someone was watching me.

One night, I woke up from my sleep. It was pitch black in my room, and my sister was sleeping on the top bunk. I felt something coming toward our beds. I couldn't see anything, but I sensed its presence. Fear came over me, and I started trembling. Feeling a presence right beside my bed, I quickly pulled the covers over my head. I was too scared to look and see if something was there or not. I fell asleep with the covers still over my head and my hands trembling.

The next night, my sister and I fell asleep in our bunk beds. That night, I woke up to our beds shaking but not too bad, though. Thinking it was my sister shaking the bed, I didn't pay any attention to it. The following night, I woke up to our beds shaking again. This time, the shaking was a little more than before.

I called my sister's name and asked her, "Are you shaking the bed?"

"No!" she said.

I went back to sleep.

A couple of nights passed, and then one night, I woke to another shaking of our beds. This time, my sister felt it.

"Doreen, did you feel that?" I called out to her.

"I sure did!" she replied.

We ran into our parents' room and slept in their beds. A few hours later, I woke up to their bed shaking. My mom, dad, and sister didn't feel it because they were sound asleep. But, I knew what was going on.

A couple of months passed. I was in my bed, and it was dark in my room. While looking around our room, I noticed a ghostly figure appear, sitting on the dresser with its legs crossed. I couldn't see the face, just the outline. I quickly threw the covers over my face, and that's the way I stayed until I fell asleep.

After three years in the house, my family decided to move. The landlord told us that an elderly woman had died in the house, but my sister and I knew there was more than just the spirit of the elderly woman in the house. There was an evil presence, as well.

I didn't understand why those things were happening to me and why I was the one seeing them and no one else. Because I was so young at the time, I didn't understand, but now that I'm an adult, I know it's important to use discernment when dealing with spirits.

Have you ever had an experience like this in your life, seeing and hearing things? If so, were you hesitant to share your experience with anybody because they might think you were crazy or just ate too late at night? How did you handle your experience?

When I Was Seventeen

In 1987, at the age of seventeen, I started going to church with my friends. One day while in my bedroom watching Jimmy Swaggart on television, I gave my life to Christ. Tired of feeling empty and like I had no purpose, I prayed and asked God to come into my heart. As I began studying God's words, it was like food for my soul. God opened my spirit to his words, and I couldn't get enough. I needed it and welcomed more.

Fast forward. The pastor at the church I attended was an older man in his 70s. At times, he would mistreat people in the church, and his actions would make the church members question if he should even be a man of God.

One night, the church had a meeting, but I decided not to go. While at home, I fell asleep and had a dream that I was in a church meeting. The pastor was claiming to be God, and it caused the church to split. The next day I spoke to one of the church members and shared my dream with her. That's when she told me it sounded like I was there because that's what had happened. My jaw dropped in disbelief.

The church divided, and so hurt, I decided not to go to church anymore. I asked God what the purpose was for going to church if people were going to act the way they do. I cried for my heart was sad.

The Lord spoke to my heart and asked, "WHAT ARE YOU

GOING TO CHURCH TO DO, WORSHIP MAN OR WORSHIP ME?"

I was excited that He spoke to me.

"You're right, Lord," I said. "I go to worship You."

After leaving that church, I found another church that I liked. Ever since the Lord spoke to my heart, I've been going to church. I still encountered bad things in the churches because there is no perfect church. But, of course, not all churches are wrong in their teachings. There's always going to be bad apples in the bunch; you have to keep searching for that good apple. Whatever you do, please don't let my experiences stop you from going to church.

The church is a group of broken people who need a savior, Jesus Christ. Some people who belong to a church put the clergy on a pedestal like they can't do any wrong. Just because Jesus was a person who did no wrong, why do people think we, as humans, won't mess up? Jesus was flawless; we are flawed. When I was a new Christian, I saw a pastor and other members smoking cigarettes. I was dumbfounded. Because they were older in the faith, I put them on a pedestal. When I saw them partake in their worldly habits, it made me look at them differently. Needless to say, I never went back to that church.

However, what I failed to realize back then was no church or person on this earth will ever be perfect. I came across a man at a previous job, and we started talking about God and church. He once was a believer in Christ until someone in the church hurt him. He was a new Christian, and he looked at them as flawless, which resulted in him ending up hurt. He didn't tell me what happened, but whatever happened caused him to lose faith in Christ. Now he's a follower of Satan. I told him what happened to me and what the Lord told me. He replied by saying he was happy serving his new master.

"It won't be for long," I told him. "When your leader calls for your soul, then what?"

Yes, Satan has the power to give all the kingdoms of this world to people if they bow down and worship him.

Again, the devil took him to a very high mountain and showed him all the kingdoms of the world and their splendor. ⁹"All this I will give you," he said, "if you will bow down and worship me." ¹⁰Jesus said to him, "Away from me, Satan! For it is written: 'Worship the Lord your God, and serve him only.'"

Matthew 4:8-10 NIV

For what shall it profit a man, if he shall gain the whole world, and loses his own soul? ³⁷Or what shall a man give in exchange for his soul?

Mark 8:36-37 KJV

There is no age requirement to follow Jesus Christ. As a follower of Christ, we have to be careful not to fall for the devil's tricks because they don't last, but God's love does. I also believe when God's children's faith falls, we are to help them understand that what they are going through is not God's fault, but they can be delivered from it.

The worldly materials and powers Satan gives are only temporary, not forever like Jesus Christ. However, a church can grow and learn the more profound things of Jesus Christ if they allow the Holy Spirit to work and change their lives. I would rather be poor and happy in Christ, knowing I will live

17

forever in peace and love, than be rich and own the world and end up in the lake of fire miserable forever.

No matter what you are going through, don't lose hope. Surround yourself with people who are positive role models. When you are a new Christian, you tend to cleave to people in the church because you don't want to be alone, and you have this spiritual hunger, and you want to know more about God from those who've been in the church for a long time and know the Word. That is the way I was, but not every believer is the same. I had to trust people, even though they make mistakes. For those who mistreated me, I just left them alone and only dealt with those who genuinely cared about me.

I was around people who sucked the joy out of me. They were always complaining and cynical, but I needed to stay away from people like that. Just like those family members who are toxic, we still love them. You will come across people in the church who act worldly. Remember, Satan is also in the church. That's why we need discernment of spirit.

Have you experienced someone acting out of their normal behavior? How did you handle their treatment of you? When this happens, pray for them and ask God to remove the negativity from their heart and spirit. Still, treat them with love.

As a new Christian believer, you are a baby in Christ. Starting out, you'll learn about who Jesus is, baptism, faith, and how to understand His words. As you keep reading, praying, and fasting, you will become a teen in God's words. Then, as an adult, you get into the deeper things of God. That's the exciting part! All of God's words are exciting and wonderful. When God starts to talk to you, you will feel his presence when He's in the room.

Brothers, I could not address you as spiritual, but as worldly—as infants in Christ. [2]I gave you milk, not solid food, for you were not yet ready for solid food. In fact, you are still not ready, [3]for you are still worldly. For since there are jealousy and dissension among you, are you not worldly? Are you not walking in the way of man? [4]For when one of you says, "I follow Paul," and another, "I follow Apollos," are you not mere men?

1 Corinthians 3:1-4 BSB

Something in the Walls

September 1987

In the dream, I was traveling headfirst down a long, circular tunnel, which was dimly lit. There was still enough light to see my surroundings, though. The walls went from being translucent to thick material. I was traveling so fast through the tunnel that I couldn't make out what was on the walls. However, while heading downward, it's like my eyes slowed the motion of my speed so I could catch a glimpse of what I saw: living bodies embedded in the walls. They were moving as if struggling to break free, but they couldn't. I couldn't see any concrete; it was like the bodies made up the entire walls.

As I continued downward, the dream changed. I was in a dark area, but in the distance, I saw a golden gate. The gate resembled the front gate at Crown Hill Cemetery on the eastside of Indianapolis, Indiana. I am not saying the gate at Crown Hill Cemetery is the gate of hell. NO! I thought I was in heaven, but then I had to remind myself that paradise isn't dark. All of a sudden, WHOOSH! I was near the gate, but no one was there. As I stood there looking inside, I noticed a man and woman coming towards the gate. Their clothes were dirty and had burn holes in them. Then more people approached the gate.

A man who was holding a pail walked toward the gate and

said in a raspy voice, "Bring us water so we can cool our tongues."

Am I really seeing this? I said to myself. At that moment, I woke up drenched in sweat. If I keep having dreams like this, I'm going to end up dehydrated, I thought while laughing at myself, the whole time my heart was beating out of my chest.

When I gave my life to Christ, I came to Him out of fear. There is nothing wrong with that; some people need the hell scared out of them to change. My fear came from the thought that if I died that day, hell would have been my home until Judgment Day, and all because I wanted to do my own thing, make my own rules, and live life my way. I didn't want to go to hell, but I knew that's where I was headed if I didn't accept Jesus Christ's invitation to give my life to Him.

As I learned more about Christ, I started learning more about His love and how much He loves me and wants to save me so I can be with Him forever. That is what changed my life, and He can change yours. Just give Him your heart and repent with all of your heart.

God is a father who chastises His children because He knows they can do better. He sends people to speak to us about Christ's love so we can be put back on the right path, to help us better understand Him, and to answer our questions at times.

Have you been asked to do something that you feel is wrong? How did you handle it? How did it make you feel?

The Rich Man and Lazarus

[19] *"There was a rich man who was clothed in purple and fine linen and who feasted sumptuously every day. [20] And at his*

gate was laid a poor man named Lazarus, covered with sores, ²¹ who desired to be fed with what fell from the rich man's table. Moreover, even the dogs came and licked his sores. ²² The poor man died and was carried by the angels to Abraham's side. The rich man also died and was buried, ²³ and in Hades, being in torment, he lifted up his eyes and saw Abraham far off and Lazarus at his side.

²⁴ And he called out, 'Father Abraham, have mercy on me, and send Lazarus to dip the end of his finger in water and cool my tongue, for I am in anguish in this flame.' ²⁵ But Abraham said, 'Child, remember that you in your lifetime received your good things, and Lazarus in like manner bad things; but now he is comforted here, and you are in anguish. ²⁶ And besides all this, between us and you a great chasm, has been fixed, in order that those who would pass from here to you may not be able, and none may cross from there to us.' ²⁷ And he said, 'Then I beg you, father, to send him to my father's house— ²⁸ for I have five brothers—so that he may warn them, lest they also come into this place of torment.' ²⁹ But Abraham said, 'They have Moses and the Prophets; let them hear them.'

³⁰ And he said, 'No, father Abraham, but if someone goes to them from the dead, they will repent.' ³¹ He said to him, 'If they do not hear Moses and the Prophets, neither will they be convinced if someone should rise from the dead.'"

Luke 16:19-31 ESV

Did God Leave Me?

One day, when I was in my late 20's, I had this overpowering feeling that God's spirit left me. I know God will never leave me nor forsake me, but that day, it felt like He did. I cried and cried and cried as a close relative died. It was the most lonely, awful, horrible feeling I have ever felt in my life. Then I knew, the Lord had allowed me to experience what the people in hell are feeling, the absence of God's presence.

God's presence is not in hell. No, in hell, you feel all the guilt, sadness, anger, and despair of everything you did wrong. Even though I repented constantly, asking for forgiveness for what I had done, I still felt an emptiness. I cried out to God, asking Him what did I do that warranted this despair. I pleaded with Him, and four hours later, I started to feel his presence return. The loneliness was gone, and I felt happy again. I told Christ that I never want to feel that again. *Please don't leave me,* I prayed to Him.

Keep your lives free from the love of money and be content with what you have, because God has said, "Never will I leave you; never will I forsake you."

Hebrews 13:5 NIV

When I read this verse in the bible, I felt a lot better

knowing my Lord will never leave me. From time to time, I strayed from Him when I didn't mean to, but He will always have my hand, like a father holding his child's hand while crossing a street. It's not money itself that is evil; it's the LOVE of it that becomes the problem.

Have you experienced a time when you felt God had disappeared or didn't care for you? How did you process those feelings?

It is easy to do wrong. Christianity is for those who want to have a changed life. You have to be willing to give up some things in your life and get rid of some people who are hindering you from prospering. You can't keep having the same friends you did when you were in the world, or they will pull you back into the world unless they gave their lives to Christ. Surround yourself with people who you know are strong Christians.

"For I know the plans I have for you," declares the Lord, "plans to prosper you and not to harm you, plans to give you hope and a future."

Jeremiah 29:11 NIV

The Train of Souls

One day, while in prayer, I asked the Lord, "What is it like to die?" About a month later, I had a dream. I was lying in bed, and in the dream, I woke up and sat on the side of my bed. While sitting there, I glanced at my door. There was a force field in the doorway. When I walked over closer to it, a voice spoke and said to put my hand through it. Scared, I prayed nothing terrible would happen to my hand. Although hesitant, I put my fingers through it first. Nothing happened. Then I put my whole hand inside. When nothing happened, I decided to walk through it. As I walked through, there was pure darkness.

While trying to find a way out, I saw two red eyes, then four red eyes and sharp metal teeth. I ran for dear life. When I looked back at them, they looked like evil robots chasing me.

As I was running, I saw a lit doorway. So, I ran and jumped through it. Once I stood up, I realized I was at a train station. It was beautiful. The color was like the cream color of pearls. Simply beautiful. While standing there, I saw a train coming from a far-off distance. It began to get closer to me, and then it passed me. The train was so close that I was able to see the shapes of the people on the train. There were tall people, short people, but then I saw a very tall man. I had an odd feeling like

I knew him. As the train went past me, it turned around and passed me again but not as close as before. As I watched, the train went by and flew upward. *THAT WAS AWESOME!* I said to myself.

I stood at the train station alone, wondering what to do. All of a sudden, the doorway opened, and I could see beautiful fruits and vegetables in a grocery store. The colors were bright, which I love, and it enticed me to go through the doorway. As I went through the door, the evil robots with the red eyes were chasing me again. Then another doorway opened that led to the fruit and vegetables, and I jumped through and woke up.

The Lord was showing me what it is like when a person dies. It's like they go through a door into the next realm of life. Some will go to the dark side; they will run and be chased by demons. But, those who belong to Christ will peacefully board the train that will lead to heaven. Is there a train in heaven? I don't know, but it was a beautiful place.

One day, we will give account to what we have done in this body. So, be kind to one another and help one another, because after death is the judgment. (Hebrews 9:27) If you don't want to see the bad things you've done, repent and ask God to help you not to repeat it. You must also forgive; forgiveness is big with God. It's not something that you learn to do overnight, although it can be. It may even take some years to get to that point, depending on the severity of the situation. Everyone is different, though. Some may find it easier to forgive someone than others.

Have you ever done or said something to someone, then later realized you shouldn't have done or said it? Sometimes I would go back and ask the person to forgive me. Once you ask a person for their forgiveness, the ball is in their court as to whether or not they forgive you. Even if they don't forgive you, you our Father in heaven forgives you. Now, forgive yourself and move on. You have a life to live.

[14]For if you forgive other people when they sin against you, your heavenly Father will also forgive you. [15]But if you do not forgive others their sins, your Father will not forgive your sins.

Matthew 6: 14-15 NIV

[31]"But when the Son of Man comes in His glory, and all the angels with Him, then He will sit on His glorious throne. [32]All the nations will be gathered before Him; and He will separate them from one another, as the shepherd separates the sheep from the goats; [33] and He will put the sheep on His right, and the goats on the left.

[34]"Then the King will say to those on His right, 'Come, you who are blessed of My Father, inherit the kingdom prepared for you from the foundation of the world. [35]For I was hungry, and you gave Me something to eat; I was thirsty, and you gave Me something to drink; I was a stranger, and you invited Me in; [36]naked, and you clothed Me; I was sick, and you visited Me; I was in prison, and you came to Me.' [37]Then the righteous will answer Him, 'Lord, when did we see You hungry, and feed You, or thirsty, and give You something to drink? [38]And when did we see You a stranger, and invite You in, or naked, and clothe You? [39]When did we see You sick, or in prison, and come to You?' [40]The King will answer and say to them, 'Truly I say to you, to the extent that you did it to one of these brothers of Mine, even the least of them, you did it to Me.'

29

[41] *"Then He will also say to those on His left, 'Depart from Me, accursed ones, into the eternal fire which has been prepared for the devil and his angels; [42] for I was hungry, and you gave Me nothing to eat; I was thirsty, and you gave Me nothing to drink; [43] I was a stranger, and you did not invite Me in; naked, and you did not clothe Me; sick, and in prison, and you did not visit Me.' [44] Then they themselves also will answer, 'Lord, when did we see You hungry, or thirsty, or a stranger, or naked, or sick, or in prison, and did not [a]take care of You?' [45] Then He will answer them, 'Truly I say to you, to the extent that you did not do it to one of the least of these, you did not do it to Me.' [46] These will go away into eternal punishment, but the righteous into eternal life."*

Matthew 25:31-46

Have you ever asked or prayed for something or someone, but it goes wrong? Were you specific in your prayers? When you asked for it, were you truly prepared for the answer?

Judgment Day

September 1999

As I was sleeping, a dream came to me. I was in a large arena with more seats than I could count. Many seats were empty, and others were filled. I didn't know what was going on. All I knew was Jesus was there. I began to hear uncontrollable crying and uncontrollable joy in the areas. At that moment, I realized it was my judgment day.

For we must all appear before the judgment seat of Christ; that every one may receive the things done in his body, according to that he hath done, whether it be good or bad.
2 Corinthians 5:10 KJV

Jesus proceeded from row to row, saying, "You may go" and "You cannot go." Then Jesus came to my aisle. My heart started pounding harder and faster. Thinking about all the things I did and didn't do in my life, I prayed to the Lord that I would be found worthy to go to heaven. Then Jesus was in the back two rows from my family and me. It was my husband at the time, one of his nephews, and my children.

From behind us, I heard a lady crying hard, and then I heard Jesus tell her, "You cannot go."

Perspiration drenched me, and my legs were shaking. Then

Jesus finally came to my row.

He smiled and said, "You may go."

I shouted with joy as I jumped up and ran to the elevator, relieved that we were going to heaven. The elevator came, the doors opened, and we all stepped inside. It was breathtakingly beautiful. As we were ascending, I looked up and saw a golden key floating in the air. I wondered what the key went to, but just as I began to reach up to grab it, I woke up.

What do you believe is your purpose in life? Do you feel you are living in your purpose? If not, what are you doing to find your purpose? What steps are you taking to step into your purpose?

The Judgment at Christ's Coming

[5]*This is evidence of the righteous judgment of God, that you may be considered worthy of the kingdom of God, for which you are also suffering—*[6]*since indeed God considers it just to repay with affliction those who afflict you,* [7]*and to grant relief to you who are afflicted as well as to us, when the Lord Jesus is revealed from heaven with his mighty angels* [8]*in flaming fire, inflicting vengeance on those who do not know God and on those who do not obey the gospel of our Lord Jesus.* [9]*They will suffer the punishment of eternal destruction, away from the presence of the Lord and from the glory of his might,* [10]*when he comes on that day to be glorified in his saints and to be marveled at among all who have believed because our testimony to you was believed.* [11]*To this end we always pray for you, that our God may make you worthy of his calling and may fulfill every resolve for good and every work of faith by his power,* [12]*so that the name of our Lord Jesus may be*

glorified in you, and you in him, according to the grace of our
God and the Lord Jesus Christ.

2 Thessalonians 1:5-12 ESV

Everyone will have to answer for their works done on Earth. God has the final say if you make it into heaven. Take a survey of what you've done with the life He has given you. Pray that He will reveal your heart so you can repent and change your course.

Get to know Christ before you leave this earth. On Judgment Day, you will see all you have done in this body and this life. Every word you speak will be judged. Do what is right; make your wrongs into right, forgive yourself, and forgive others. If you can't forgive others for their sins against you, God will not forgive you of your sins.

But I say unto you, That every idle word that men shall speak,
they shall give account thereof in the day of judgment.

Matthew 12:36 KJB

"Idle word" means empty rhetoric or insincere or exaggerated talk. Simply, they are words full of sound and fury, signifying nothing.

My Daughter

I got married when I was twenty-five years old. When I turned twenty-six, I got pregnant with my first child. Three months into my pregnancy, I started having complications. So, we went to the ER, but the baby died in my womb. The nurse administered medication to help me go into labor, and when I pushed, the baby came out in the amniotic sac that looked like a little water balloon. When the nurse asked me if I wanted to see it, I responded yes, and she burst the sac so I could see the baby better. Because it was an embryo, it hadn't fully developed. So, we never knew the sex of the child. Heartbroken, I cried uncontrollably for a few weeks while recovering from the lost, I prayed for God to reveal the sex of my child.

Five months later, I dreamed of children of all nationalities playing in an area that looked like a playground. It was awesome to see hundreds of beautiful children, each wearing their native clothing. There were children from India, Africa, Asia, and several other countries. I watched and laughed as they played. Then I noticed a black lady sitting on the grass with a child on her lap. Other women were sitting with children on their laps, as well, waiting to show the next parent their child or children they had lost, who asked the same question that I did: "God, was it a boy or a girl?"

Then, a voice spoke to me. "Look down."

As I looked down at the child sitting on the lady's lap, the child's eyes fixed on mine. The child was a little girl. Her hair was a mess, with stuff all over her head from playing. Suddenly, she gave me the biggest grin. *OH, MY GOSH! She looks just like my son when he was little,* I said to myself. She even had the same smile, only with girlish features.

While looking at her, a voice spoke to me and said, "This is the answer to your question."

I woke up crying and thanking Jesus for letting me know the sex of the baby who I lost. When I saw her, she looked to be around five or six years old. God is amazing!

One time, I heard this minister speak about a friend of his who had a near-death experience. She went to a children's heaven and saw massive amounts of children, almost the same as I did. But, she told the minister that the Lord has treehouses for them to live and play in, and they all live together. My heart was filled with joy because I now know I was in the children's heaven.

I believe when infants and children die, they go back to God. If you lost a little one, rest assured they are in heaven. All the near-death experiences I've heard, not one person has mentioned seeing children in hell. They have witnessed teenagers in hell, but no babies or children. I haven't seen any children or babies in the dreams and visions that I've had of hell either.

Also, if you decided to abort a child, there is still hope. God still loves you! Repent, forgive yourself, and move on. He's a

God of many chances. But, moving forward, practice safe sex, or stay sexually abstinent until God blesses you with the person whom you want to have a child by. If you are a woman who has had many miscarriages, and you think God is not going to bless you with a child, don't believe the hype that Satan is whispering in your ears. God will open your womb in His time.

A friend of mine thought she couldn't have a child. She was married with no children. They wanted to have a baby but couldn't. For years, the doctors told her that she couldn't have children. So, they adopted a baby boy. After their son grew up to be an adult, she divorced her husband, and they moved on with their lives. My friend then met a man, and things got serious between them. During one of her doctor visits, she learned she was pregnant. Of course, she didn't believe it until she saw the test results. Her son is now twelve years old. God had opened her womb in His timing.

Only when God is ready, if it is His will, he will open your womb so you can bear a child. It's not in our timing; it's in God's timing. The devil will try to cause you pain to destroy you, so you'll feel like there's no hope. But there is hope! This is what you have to do. Get up, do your hair, put on makeup, slip on your most beautiful dress, and get back to living. By doing so, you'll make the devil mad because you didn't give in to depression. YOU GO, GIRL! Just like the angel told me in a dream later in this book: KEEP LOOKING UP!

Have you lost a child or know of someone who has lost a child? Do you believe they go back to God in heaven?

[13] For you formed my inward parts; you knitted me together in my mother's womb. [14] I praise you, for I am fearfully and wonderfully made. Wonderful are your works; my soul knows it very well. [15] My frame was not hidden from you, when I was being made in secret, intricately woven in the depths of the earth. [16] Your eyes saw my unformed substance; in your book were written, every one of them, the days that were formed for me, when as yet there was none of them.

Psalm 139:13-16 ESV

People Walking in My Hallway

June 2001

My son was four years old when I rented half of a duplex on the south side of town in Indianapolis, Indiana. It was a lovely home with three bedrooms, one full bathroom, and a half bath. The rooms were upstairs, and the stairs were so steep that I was afraid for my son to walk up or down them. I feared he would fall to his death if he lost his footing. It also had a basement, which I didn't like. I never went down there because it was dreadfully eerie.

One night, I was turning off all the lights downstairs. The stairwell was somewhat dark but not too dark to the point where you couldn't see. When I turned to the stairway, I saw a little child sitting on the steps.

Thinking it was my son, I said, "Go upstairs. I'll be up there shortly."

I turned away for only a few seconds to make sure all the lights were off, and when I looked back at the stairs, the child was gone.

What the hell did I see? I said to myself. *I would've heard my son going up the stairs.*

When I called for my son, he responded, "I'm upstairs in my room."

WHAT? I internally screamed.

*****

Three months passed, and a friend needed a place to stay. So, I allowed her to stay with us.

One night, she asked me, "Do you know your son sleepwalks?"

Having no clue, I replied, "No!"

"He came into my room and went to the corner," she told me. "He looked like he needed to use the bathroom, so I took him to the bathroom and then laid him back down in his room."

"Oh, okay," I said, then thanked her.

Sleepwalking can be scary and can also cause the person harm. Afraid he would fall down the stairs while sleepwalking, I went and got him out of his bed and put him in my bed. I thought if he got up, I would feel the bed shake.

Something did wake me, but it wasn't my son getting out of the bed. I sat up and stared straight ahead at the doorway. I was in a trance. Suddenly, I started to see people walking up and down my hallway. There were many of them. As I stared at them, I thought to myself, *Where are all these people coming from?*

As I continued looking on, I noticed they weren't actually walking in the hallway. Wherever they were was being projected into that dark space. They were walking as if they were tired, and their expressions were sad. The people were all races, shapes, and sizes, but one woman's image was so clear to me. She was a white woman wearing a light green polka-dot dress, and she had her hair in a bun. She looked like she was from the 1800's era or so, I would assume.

As I looked on, someone from the other side saw me and tried to touch me, as if they wanted to know if I was a real person. There appeared to be a force field between us because when they reached out to try to touch me, I saw the imprint from their baby finger to the first finger. That's when I cried out, "THE BLOOD OF JESUS!" Instantly, everything returned to normal, and the people disappeared. Although shaken by what I had just witnessed, I laid down to go back to sleep in peace.

This vision was clear, and there were so many people. They didn't have burnt holes in their clothes nor were they dirty. It was like when you are in a courtroom and waiting on the verdict, not knowing what's going to happen. No one was talking to one another; they just looked in a daze. If there is a holding place, and I'm not saying there is such a place, I believe that was it.

Give your life to Christ so you will not end up in that place of darkness and despair. It's much better to be with Christ, where there is light, peace, and the son of God. In the next life, we will talk to one another, fellowship, and have a new body. I'm looking forward to that day. I'm going to go all over the world, sit with the animals, and play with them. It will be a glorious day.

Have you experienced a time when something has happened to you, but it's hard to explain it? How were you able to process it? What did you do to protect yourself?

Tell Them I'm Coming Soon!

January 2008

I laid down to take a nap, and I started dreaming that a group of people and I were standing in an open field. There was chaos happening in different areas of the world, but where I was at was peaceful. Suddenly, I disappeared and was placed upon a mountain behind a large rock.

After I disappeared, the sky turned red, and the ground cracked open. Lava shot up through the cracks in the concrete. Cars turned over; people were running. It was pure chaos. People were dying from either the lava or from being trampled by those who were trying to flee. It was sheer madness as I looked on.

Beside me stood a man, who I felt was my best friend. When I asked him what was going on, he replied, "Your disappearance represents the Rapture, and the chaos you saw was the Tribulation." Then he said, "Tell my people I'm coming soon."

When I thought about this dream, I said, "Oh my gosh! Lord, that was actually you!" I started crying because He had chosen me to send his angel to and to show me things that were going to happen. I don't know how it happens, but He shows His people things before they happen.

That's how much He loves us. God loves us so much that He sent His son to die for you and me. God is telling us that He is coming back for sure and to get on board before it's too late. God doesn't want to destroy people nor the earth, but there has to be punishment for sin because mankind is so stubborn, selfish, hard of heart, and wants to be their own god.

Unlike judges here on Earth who will send a person to jail for stealing, killing, or breaking any other law, Jesus died so that we don't have to be punished by breaking God's commandments. His death on the cross allowed us to commune with God ourselves. We can go to God and ask for forgiveness ourselves. I don't have to confess my sins to a man so he can ask God to forgive me. I bow to my knees and ask the Lord Jesus Christ to forgive me for all my sins, to help me in my weaknesses, and to keep His protection around my family and me. I talk to God like He is right in front of me. I've argued, yelled, and was very angry with Him but later asked Him to forgive me for yelling at Him. But that's the beauty of knowing Christ; He knows our hearts.

I believe the Lord showed me what will soon take place on the earth one day. He told me to tell you about this dream of the calamity and His soon return. There is no one like our God. He tells His people ahead of time so that we won't be caught off guard. Only those who are not looking and waiting for His coming will be caught off guard. I am a watchman on the wall. When I see danger coming, I give a warning. You can believe it or not believe it. Just like in Lot's time, some of his family didn't believe him, and some of his children were destroyed when fire reigned on Sodom and Gomorrah (Genesis 19).

Have you experienced a time where you just missed a car

accident or another devastating event because you were late? How did this make you feel?

¹⁶*For God so loved the world that he gave his only Son, that whoever believes in him should not perish but have eternal life.* ¹⁷*For God did not send his Son into the world to condemn the world, but in order that the world might be saved through him.* ¹⁸*Whoever believes in him is not condemned, but whoever does not believe is condemned already, because he has not believed in the name of the only Son of God.*

John 3:16-18 ESV

Fly Away

March 12, 2009

In a dream, I was standing in an outside parking lot with no cars. I remember seeing the lines outlining the empty spaces. It was daylight, and my feet were on the ground. Then, I started going up in the air like a rocket. The sensation in the pit of my stomach was similar to the feeling when you are taking off in an airplane. I smiled as I looked up, but when I looked down, I got scared as I watched the ground get smaller and smaller the higher I went. Then, it was completely white. Soon, I saw misty blue skies, and eventually, I started seeing people flying about. Three people were on my right side, two on my left. They were holding each other's arms as they ascended.

When wondering what was going on, I was held back while still in the sky, and I saw a bigger scene. I saw hundreds of people going up in the air. All in all, it was glorious.

[13]But we do not want you to be uninformed, brothers, about those who are asleep, that you may not grieve as others do who have no hope. [14]For since we believe that Jesus died and rose again, even so, through Jesus, God will bring with him those who have fallen asleep. [15]For this we declare to you by a word from the Lord, that we who are alive, who are left until the coming of the Lord, will not precede those who have fallen asleep. [16]For the Lord himself will descend from heaven with

a cry of command, with the voice of an archangel, and with the sound of the trumpet of God. And the dead in Christ will rise first. [17]Then we who are alive, who are left, will be caught up together with them in the clouds to meet the Lord in the air, and so we will always be with the Lord. [18]Therefore encourage one another with these words.

1 Thessalonians 4:13-18 ESV

The Day of the Lord

[1]Now as to the times and the seasons' brethren, you have no need of anything to be written to you. [2]For you yourselves know full well that the day of the Lord will come just like a thief in the night. [3]While they are saying, "Peace and safety!" then destruction will come upon them suddenly like labor pains upon a woman with child, and they will not escape. [4]But you, brethren, are not in darkness, that the day would overtake you like a thief; [5]for you are all sons of light and sons of day. We are not of night nor of darkness; [6]so then let us not sleep as others do, but let us be alert and sober. [7]For those who sleep do their sleeping at night, and those who get drunk get drunk at night. [8]But since we are of the day, let us be sober, having put on the breastplate of faith and love, and as a helmet, the hope of salvation. [9]For God has not destined us for wrath, but for obtaining salvation through our Lord Jesus Christ, [10]who died for us, so that whether we are awake or asleep, we will live together with Him. [11]Therefore encourage one another and build up one another, just as you are doing.

1 Thessalonians 5:1-11 NASB

Do you want to be a part of the great gathering?

King David

I was walking back from the desert with a man. He brought King David a gift of fine foods from afar, and King David was pleased. Then I sat down with my mother. There was a woman whose husband was mean and angry. He would strike her so hard that she would fall to the ground. He was arguing with her because she spoke to him in public.

"How would you feel if a woman hit you?" I told him.

He stood up, came to me, and attempted to take me down a hallway, but I grabbed his manhood and squeezed as hard as I could. He screamed like a baby. I knew he was going to hit me before I grabbed them. After I released my grip, I ran to King David's table. King David's servants allowed me to sit in the second seat from King David, and I felt safe.

The man's wife was leaving. She went through the front door, and then all of a sudden, an arrow pierced her body, killing her. I knew her husband had done it. While sitting at the king's table, I told King David what had happened. Then someone slid a large yellow envelope under the king's door. The servant picked up the envelope. He was going to open it for the king, but there was a knock at the door.

I knew the envelope was from the man who wanted to hurt

me. The servants opened the door, and the man stood there with a second yellow envelope.

"That's the man who is trying to hurt me," I told the king.

King David grabbed the yellow envelope from the man who wanted to hurt me and opened it. Then he asked the man, "What is this? What do you want with our future queen?"

When I heard him refer to me as a future queen, I had to do a double-take. *WAIT! WHAT?* I thought to myself.

Then King David asked him to bow down to him, but the man refused. So, King David slammed the man on the floor. I knew it was over for him; he was going to die! I smiled as the king beat up the man. Oh, and just to let you know, King David was black and extremely handsome. If I could put a face to him today, he would look like a grown but younger version of Denzel, only more masculine in the face.

So Jesse sent for him. He was dark and handsome, with beautiful eyes. And the LORD said, "This is the one; anoint him."

1 Samuel 16:12 NLT

I felt like King David is a form of Christ protecting his bride. People will die in the process, but God will be with her and will protect the bride from the arrows Satan throws at her. Then soon, the bride will be married to the king forever.

From where do you draw your strength? When you are scared or needing help, who do you go to for help?

The Evil Eye

June 13, 2010

I was in church with a group of friends and a few other people. We were watching something on TV, and the Holy Spirit's presence was strong. Some of the people got up and started dancing in the Holy Spirit. As I looked on, I heard this guy say the apocalypse had begun. People vanished all over the world.

Then the dream switched to a carriage and horses. It was foggy and misty, and I saw a person with an evil eye. Specifically, he only had one eye, and I could only see half of his face. He was searching for Jews. Then I saw a man (a protector of children) leading this group of kids, of which some were Jewish. As the girls were walking down the sidewalk, the man knew the carriage was coming. Some Jewish girls walked ahead. While they were walking, the protector came behind and grabbed them, and hid them from the carriage to keep them safe.

This dream reminds me of the nation of Israel when they go through the seven-year tribulation, which is called Jacob's trouble. We know that Jacob's name was changed to Israel by the angel.

²²The same night he arose and took his two wives, his two female servants, and his eleven children, and crossed the ford of the Jabbok. ²³He took them and sent them across the stream, and everything else that he had. ²⁴And Jacob was left alone. And a man wrestled with him until the breaking of the day. ²⁵When the man saw that he did not prevail against Jacob, he touched his hip socket, and Jacob's hip was put out of joint as he wrestled with him. ²⁶Then he said, "Let me go, for the day has broken." But Jacob said, "I will not let you go unless you bless me." ²⁷And he said to him, "What is your name?" And he said, "Jacob." ²⁸Then he said, "Your name shall no longer be called Jacob, but Israel, for you have striven with God and with men, and have prevailed."

Genesis 32:22-28 ESV

The evil eye is Satan, and his angels will be with him. There will be angels protecting the nation of Israel, and there will come a time when the Anti-Christ will set himself up in their temple and proclaim to be God. The Jews will have to go into hiding, and while they are in hiding, God will send protectors to keep them safe.

He will oppose and will exalt himself over everything that is called God or is worshiped, so that he sets himself up in God's temple, proclaiming himself to be God.

2 Thessalonians 2:4 NIV

God is so amazing. I feel the Lord is getting his people prepared to go home but also warning the Jewish people of the coming problems. But know that for whoever will be in that timeframe, God will never leave you. Although He will provide an escape, don't live your life hoping you'll make it to heaven in the tribulation. If you can't live for Christ now, how are you going to feel when they stand you in a line to get your head chopped off because you won't take the mark?

Then I saw thrones, and they sat on them, and judgment was given to them. And I saw the souls of those who had been beheaded because of their testimony of Jesus and because of the word of God, and those who had not worshiped the beast or his image, and had not received the mark on their forehead and on their hand; and they came to life and reigned with Christ for a thousand years.

Revelation 20:4 NAS

Do you have something or someone who you feel is a danger to you? How have you protected yourself from it or them?

The Dragon

June 20, 2010

My dad was living in a senior community, and he had a caregiver. The caregiver came and took a lot of the seniors underground. I knew she was protecting them, so I didn't stop her. Shortly after, I saw people getting their guns ready, which made me curious as to what was going on.

There was military action all over the area. The men had Nazi symbols on their uniforms, and German people were there. How did I know that German people were there? I just knew in my spirit.

"What's going on?" I asked a woman named Cody.

"We are waiting to see the Messiah," she replied.

I knew she wasn't talking about Jesus Christ. Wanting to see who he was, I waited.

While waiting around, I watched through the glass door as the seniors went outside with their chairs. Looking through the door, I saw an enormous red dragon walking down the street. I continued to watch him until he was out of my view. Suddenly, a tremendous amount of heat came from the same direction the dragon had gone.

I opened the door and heard it speak, but its words were so hot, just like the heat from the sun. I'm not sure what the heat represented. I believe it was evil that was coming from the dragon. Not unless the heat was to comfort them to sleep spiritually. I couldn't handle it. I had to go back in, but it didn't faze the people on the porch who were watching and listening. I was amazed that the people could withstand so much heat.

Once it was over, a lady walked into the building like she was in a trance. She walked slowly toward a man sitting at a desk. As she was walking, I waved my hand over her eyes, but she didn't blink at all. She extended the back of her hand out to the man at the desk and said, "Give me the mark."

He seized the dragon—that old serpent, who is the devil, Satan— and bound him in chains for a thousand years.

Revelation 20:2 NLT

[16]And he causeth all, both small and great, rich and poor, free and bond, to receive a mark in their right hand, or in their foreheads: [17]And that no man might buy or sell, save he that had the mark, or the name of the beast, or the number of his name.

Revelation 13:16-17 ESV

The man at the desk gave her the mark. Scared, I ran out of the side door. Once outside, I saw loads of tanks and armed Nazi men standing around. No one could get by without someone spotting them. I was so scared. I prayed and asked God to please help me get through and to hide me so they could not see me.

As I knelt and inched my way around the tanks, I passed by two guardsmen, but they didn't see me. I escaped unseen.

And a great sign appeared in heaven: a woman clothed with the sun, with the moon under her feet, and on her head a crown of twelve stars. [2]She was pregnant and was crying out in birth pains and the agony of giving birth. [3]And another sign appeared in heaven: behold, a great red dragon, with seven heads and ten horns, and on his heads seven diadems. [4]His tail swept down a third of the stars of heaven and cast them to the earth. And the dragon stood before the woman who was about to give birth, so that when she bore her child he might devour it. [5]She gave birth to a male child, one who is to rule all the nations with a rod of iron, but her child was caught up to God and to his throne, [6]and the woman fled into the wilderness, where she has a place prepared by God, in which she is to be nourished for 1,260 days.

Revelation 12:1-6 ESV

And I saw a beast rising out of the sea, with ten horns and seven heads, with ten diadems on its horns and blasphemous names on its heads. [2]And the beast that I saw was like a leopard; its feet were like a bear's, and its mouth was like a lion's mouth. And to it the dragon gave his power and his throne and great authority. [3]One of its heads seemed to have a mortal wound, but its mortal wound was healed, and the whole earth marveled as they followed the beast. [4]And they worshiped the dragon, for he had given his authority to the beast, and they worshiped the beast, saying, "Who is like the beast, and who can fight against it?" [5]And the beast was given a mouth uttering haughty and blasphemous words, and it was allowed to exercise authority for forty-two months. [6]It opened its mouth to utter blasphemies against God, blaspheming his name and his dwelling, that is, those who dwell in heaven. [7]Also it was allowed to make war on the saints and to conquer them. And authority was given it over every tribe and people and language and nation, [8]and all who dwell on earth will worship it, everyone whose name has not been written before the foundation of the world in the book of life of the Lamb who was slain... [10]If anyone is to be taken captive, to captivity he goes; if anyone is to be slain with the sword, with the sword must he be slain. Here is a call for the endurance and faith of the saints.

Revelation 13:1-8, 10 ESV

My understanding is Satan will use hate groups to do his will, to cause chaos and confusion more so in the last days. But God is love, and He loves them, as well. However, they have a choice to follow evil or good. God is also a God of wrath; He will not tolerate evil for very long. God will make everything right again, and there will be no more evil in the world. GET RID OF SATAN! NO MORE EVIL! GO, GOD!

DO NOT TAKE THE MARK! YOU WILL LOSE YOUR SOUL. IT'S A ONE-WAY TICKET TO HELL.

You have a choice to follow evil or good. When making life's decisions, how will you decide?

Terror on Land and In the Sky

June 27, 2010

In a dream, I was on my way home from work with my son, when we saw a mushroom cloud and an explosion in the air. Radiation spread all over, but it didn't affect us. Different horrible events were happening one after the other.

The sky turned dark, and it started to hail at some point. Then daylight. Suddenly, it became tremendously dark during the day. I looked at the sky, which was breaking up, and saw ghost-like figures flying all around. Every ghost was an evil spirit.

While we were in the house, a car drove up on our lawn. I thought it was my mother, but it wasn't. The eerie thing was that the people inside the vehicle were dead, meaning they couldn't have possibly been driving the car since the dead cannot drive; it was their spirit that was dead. I had never been so afraid in my life.

Although the second coming of Christ had not happened yet, I rejoiced because I knew it was coming, and God was still protecting us. Even in my dream, I felt His presence.

I believe that dream was about the tribulation times. During that time, a lot of supernatural events will happen all over the world. The Anti-Christ, who will be Satan himself dwelling in that person, and the fallen angels will be down here, as well. That time will be literal hell on earth.

[7]And war broke out in heaven: Michael and his angels fought with the dragon; the dragon and his angels fought, [8]but they did not prevail, nor was a place found for them in heaven any longer. [9]So the great dragon was cast out, that serpent of old called the Devil and Satan, who deceives the whole world; he was cast to the earth, and his angels were cast out with him. [10]Then I heard a loud voice saying in heaven, "Now salvation, and strength, and the kingdom of our God, and the power of His Christ have come, for the accuser of our brethren, who accused them before our God day and night, has been cast down. [11]And they overcame him by the blood of the Lamb and by the word of their testimony, and they did not love their lives to the death. [12]Therefore rejoice, O heavens, and you who dwell in them! Woe to the inhabitants of the earth and the sea! For the devil has come down to you, having great wrath, because he knows that he has a short time."

Revelation 12:7-12 NKJ

My opinion is that Satan was cast out of heaven. He can roam the earth, as well, but he's able to go to God to accuse man before God. I believe when he is finally kicked out for good, where he won't be able to come back to accuse mankind before God anymore, he will be furious. He will still have control of the air because he causes fire to come down out of heaven.

Some say when Satan was kicked out, it was in the beginning? I believe it's dual, meaning it will happen twice, but the second time will be permanent. Then Satan will go after the women who are in Israel.

⁶One day the sons of God came to present themselves before the LORD, and Satan also came with them. ⁷"Where have you come from?" said the LORD to Satan. "From roaming through the earth," he replied, "and walking back and forth in it."

Job 1:6-7 BSB

"Be alert and of sober mind. Your enemy the devil prowls around like a roaring lion looking for someone to devour."

1 Peter 5:8 NIV

⁹Then Satan answered the LORD and said, "Does Job fear God for no reason? ¹⁰Have You not put a hedge around him and his house and all that he has, on every side? You have blessed the work of his hands, and his possessions have increased in the land. ¹¹But stretch out Your hand and strike all that he has, and he will curse You to Your face."

Job 1:9-11 NLT

In our lives, it may feel like one destruction after another, but sometimes, it is a test of our faith and patience. Every situation is different. God had a hedge around Job, who was a praying man. I believe prayers are what strengthens that hedge. So, when adverse events happen, pray for God's protection.

Boulder Storm

December 14, 2010

I remember exiting the front doors of the hotel where I worked. My friend, Tina, was meeting me for lunch, and she wanted me to hurry and get there because a storm was coming.

Upon stepping outside, I looked up and saw a formation of black, lumpy-looking rocks in the sky. They looked little at first, but as they got closer and started hitting the land, I saw that they were much larger. Flaming rocks began flying everywhere, and people were running to avoid them. I told them to get inside as the storm grew worse.

As I rushed people inside, it started raining heavily, which caused flooding. The waters rushed through the hotel's front doors, and then just as quickly as it started, it stopped. No more falling rocks or rain. The sky was clear for a couple of hours or so. However, as people headed out of the hotel, it started again. This time, huge boulders were falling. Remember the movie *Indiana Jones* when he was in the cave and a massive stone started rolling behind him? Well, that's the size of the boulders that were falling from the sky.

The hotel supervisor tried to get inside, but a boulder smashed him against a wall. I cried while making my way downstairs to the basement to hide with the many others, hoping and praying for the storm to stop.

And great hailstones, about one hundred pounds each, fell from heaven on people; and they cursed God for the plague of the hail because the plague was so severe.

Revelation 16:21 ESV

[24]But in those days, after that tribulation, the sun will be darkened, and the moon will not give its light, [25]and the stars will be falling from heaven, and the powers in the heavens will be shaken. [26]And then they will see the Son of Man coming in clouds with great power and glory.

Mark 13:24-26 ESV

When the time comes, you won't be able to hide. However, you should pray. Prepare your hearts and accept Christ in your life. We are not promised tomorrow.

The Two Sisters

My sister and I were living in an apartment together. The era was the 18th century. Our apartment was on the first floor, so we were close to the street. There were plans to develop real estate in the area. This day, the people came and were blasting through the mountain with explosives to start the first phase.

Some residents didn't want to sell to help develop the area, but that didn't deter those people who said they would develop around us. As they cleared the streets, the blasting started. Obviously, someone didn't know what he was doing, because when the blast went off, it hit our apartment and others nearby.

My sister was taking a shower when it happened. I ran to the bathroom to find her unconscious. After pulling her out, I called her name, but she didn't wake up. So, I slapped her on the face, and she opened her eyes.

When the next blast happened, the floor raised, and I could look down to the next level below me. It looked like I was over a small volcano because all I could see were flames.

After my sister finally got up from the floor, we proceeded to go outside. While outside, I spoke very loudly and forcefully to the people. No one liked each other. They were cursing at one another and spewing hate.

Once my sister and I went back inside the apartment, we sat at the kitchen table.

"Let's go back home," my sister suggested, and I agreed.

Both of us were in the bedroom and packing our belongings when we heard another blast. This time, it created a tsunami, which knocked us unconscious.

When we woke up, other people were in our apartment. I opened the door. My sister and I were in an office room with people filling out applications for jobs. The office area was updated to a modern style as we went forward in time.

"How did we get here?" I asked.

I noticed no one was looking at us, and when we spoke to them, no one responded.

We're dead! That's why no one can see us, I thought to myself.

The two sisters died in the tsunami.

In this dream, I was looking through the eyes of two sisters. They were two Caucasian women, but I saw them as my sister and me. I don't know who they were, but they lived back in the 18th century and died in a tsunami.

After the tsunami, the two sisters woke up in a different century, and their old apartment had been turned into an office building where people were hired for jobs.

I didn't know when they started doing blasting in history, but after doing some research, this is what I found on Wikipedia online: *On this day in 1869, the presidents of the Union Pacific and Central Pacific railroads meet in Promontory, Utah, and drive a ceremonial last spike into a rail line that connects their railroads. This made transcontinental railroad travel possible for the first time in U.S. history. The history of nitroglycerin*

66

and the Central Pacific Railroad is an interesting one, as much has been made of the many workers killed using this new explosive in the building of the Pacific Railroad. Nitroglycerine was invented in 1846 by Ascanio Sobrero. Albert Nobel designed a blasting cap that made use of the explosive almost safe in 1865, and in 1867, Nobel mixed silica and nitroglycerine, making dynamite. Prior to 1867, nitroglycerine was shipped as a liquid; the first known specimen of this liquid was reported in California on April 21, 1866, in a newspaper article in the Placer Herald, Auburn, California.

This blew my mind. What I found interesting is the dream was in the 1800s.

Mechanical Terror

June 2013

It was a lovely day with beautiful blue skies, and I was outside with some friends. All of a sudden, a long, mechanical-looking worm came through the clouds, and another came along after it. They started to burst through the clouds one after another. Then these creatures began killing the humans. They were like little robots, eliminating human life all over. We took everything we could find to kill them. It was like we were fighting robots from a movie.

While I was fighting one, a huge transformer-like creature came from the middle of the sky; it was a centipede or worm-like kind of machine. Before it could hit the earth, I turned and saw Jesus in the sky.

"YES! ABOUT TIME!" I yelled.

Tired of fighting those robots, I started rejoicing and praising Jesus. It was his second coming, and everyone saw him. Then I woke up in a pool of sweat.

I don't know if these types of mechanical weapons are going to happen, but the Lord did say that knowledge will increase in the last days. I wouldn't be surprised if they had something like it made.

Please don't miss His first coming, the rapture, as the Bible speaks about his second coming where every eye will see him.

Look! He comes with the clouds of heaven, and everyone will see him — even those who pierced him. And all the nations of the world will mourn for him. Yes! Amen!

Revelations 1:7 NLT

Ask yourself if you want to do whatever you want to do and miss the rapture? Or will you accept Christ, live by His laws, get baptized, repent daily, and do your best to live by His words so that you won't be left behind? The choice is yours.

The Men in the Middle

August 2013

One day, while in prayer, I asked God to allow me to see an angel, but in a human form and not so tall that it would scare me. A couple of months passed, and I had a dream of being at the Alamo in Texas. I've never been there and only seen pictures of the place.

While standing around looking at the sights, I saw groups of people in white robes. They were marching in a circular pattern close to one another like they were protecting someone. Two men in the middle were talking to each other. One was tall and the other short. I wanted to know what was happening, so I started walking towards them.

They aren't going to let me through, I thought to myself, but as I began to walk into the circle of people, they allowed me through. I heard the short guy tell the tall guy that they must go and visit someone. In my dream, he spoke the name of the person, but I can't remember it. In my spirit, it was the name of a king.

As I got closer to the two men, I could see that the tall guy was on a pedestal, almost like when an athlete receives their medal during the Olympics. They were on a stair-like stage, and the tall guy was dressed in a black suit.

I thought to myself, *Is this the devil?* However, as I got closer, I noticed he had on a white priest collar.

After approaching him, I asked, "What is going on?"

When I said that, he bent down and looked at me. His face was close to mine, almost to the point I could kiss him. As I looked at him, I had a weird but good feeling, and it had something to do with his eyes, which were full of peace. His pupils were dark but just in the middle, not all over. It was like he was in a black and white picture. I couldn't look away; I was drawn to him.

When he started speaking to me, his language was Hebrew, but I heard it as English. He said many things that I don't remember. As he was talking, I felt my eyes close, and for a moment, I saw stars as if I were in space. Then as I was coming out of my sleep, I experienced an overwhelming feeling of pure love that I had never known before nor felt from any human on this earth. It was a reminder of how much God loves me. But He doesn't just love me; He truly loves all the people in this world.

I woke up crying like I had lost a loved one, but they were tears of joy and happiness that no man on Earth could give or show me. I knew God had allowed me to feel the love that He has for us, no doubt. I wish everyone could feel the love that I felt in the dream. It was God himself that let me feel His heart for us. Have you ever had an overwhelming feeling while dreaming and knew it was real?

Seek God and experience his love for yourself. The more you read His words in the Bible, the closer He will become, and you will be able to experience His love on a personal level for yourself. IT'S AMAZING!

Seal the Door

April 2, 2014

There was a room filled with TVs. It almost looked like a security room, but Satan was watching the screens. Chaos from all over the world was being broadcasted on TV monitors. Each TV had a disaster happening in different countries. When I passed the room, I looked back and saw a monstrous hand trying to grab me. In the dream, my sister appeared next to me, as if she had always been there. My sister and I started pleading the blood of Christ over the door. We called the name of Jesus, and He came and placed a seal over the door with a flaming sword. I remember when God placed a flaming sword to keep Adam and Eve out of the garden.

Satan sees the destruction that goes on in the earth, and he is the cause of some.

Be alert and of sober mind. Your enemy the devil prowls around like a roaring lion looking for someone to devour.

1 Peter 5:8 NIV

No matter what happens in life, God will be there to help and protect you, if it is His will. Trust in His name and plead the blood against the enemies of God.

Hadassah Cohen

Jesus saith unto him, I am the way, the truth, and the life: no man cometh unto the Father but by me.

John 14:6 KJV

Jesus also said, "I am the door," found in John 10:7, and this statement is third of the seven "I AM" declarations of Jesus recorded only in John's Gospel. These "I AM" proclamations point to His unique, divine identity and purpose. In this "I AM" statement, Jesus points out for us the exclusive nature of salvation by saying that He is *"the"* door, not *"a"* door. Furthermore, Jesus is not only our Shepherd, who leads us into the "sheepfold," but He is the only door by which we may enter and be saved (John 10:9). Jesus is the only means we have of receiving eternal life (John 3:16). There is no other way.

The Big Smile

February 2015

In the dream, I was walking across a bridge that had a gate at the end of it. When I got to the gate, there was a man. He asked my name, and I told him. Then I looked up at the heavens and saw a big smile with teeth. It was God smiling at me, and I smiled back.

"You may go in," the man at the gate replied.

When I went in, the place was breathtaking! It was absolutely beautiful! I can't remember much of the details about how it looked, but I know the streets were made of gold.

As I walked around, there was a birthday party going on, and I saw Jesus as a little boy. God stood next to Jesus. Of course, God is a spirit, but when I saw *Hercules* (the cartoon), Hercules's dad is who I pictured God to look like because of his beard and white hair, even though they are characters in the Greek mythology. I'm not saying I believe in the Greek gods, but that's what I pictured God to look like in my mind. Jesus was so cute, jumping up and down in his chair. I waved to the kids and my daughter at the party before proceeding on.

While walking, I started seeing items of the earth encased in glass. This stuff was from the '70s and '80s. "I remember that," I said to myself while looking inside of the 80's area as I passed the glass. As I continued to walk, it was like I was entering an old school hallway. Then I saw a door that had letters on it that spelled out "Office".

"I'm going to make an appointment to see God," I told myself.

I walked into a massive room that had a long chalkboard. Nobody was in the room, and there was nothing written on the chalkboard. Then I saw a door that led into an office. As soon as I reached to touch the knob, I heard people inside the room. When I looked back, there was writing on the board. I turned and walked towards the board to read the names and dates written on it. They listed those living and those who died. A man was standing by the board, and I asked him about what was on the board. However, when he opened his mouth to respond, a lady who was near him started waving her arms while trying to cover the information so I couldn't see the chalkboard.

"She should not see this! She can't see this!" the lady voiced loudly to the man as she continued waving her arms.

Is this real? I thought to myself.

As I got closer to the board, I saw various names; some seemed to be from different cultures. There was one name I noticed, though. The person had a long last name, and it ended in 'ski'. He had already died. The names at the bottom were the ones who were going to die. I saw the dates, but I can't remember them. When I saw their names, it made me sad, and I started crying.

My daughter came to me and said, "Momma, can you stay?"

"I can't," I told her while crying. "I must go back."

She was sad. I was sad, as well.

Live every day like it's your last. Make the most of each day, and always keep Christ first. Surround yourself with positive people, and stay away from those who are negative and suck the joy out of you. Live your life for Christ. Love people like Christ. Love yourself.

Going into the Red

Pastor Perry Stone said he saw in a vision of five cities burning. I remember one that the Lord showed me in 2015. I saw five bubbles; each contained a vision of events that were happening in the world. As I watched the chaos, a speedometer appeared like those equipped in a car, and the needle was racing to the red. Before the vision ended, the needle had already reached the first small red mark of the red zone. There were three more markings before it reached the largest red mark.

No one wants to believe we are on the brink of a global collapse. The Bible already told us these things are coming and not to be afraid. I still have some things I want to do in this life, but he told us to LOOK UP BECAUSE OUR REDEMPTION IS DRAWING NEAR! However, the prophecies have to come to pass whether we like it or not. Just because you don't want to see, it won't stop it.

Put your trust in the Lord. He is the only one that can keep you at peace in the storm.

The Bride

March 2015

In March of 2015, I had a dream I was working at Walmart. It was around my son's birthday in September, and I was getting married. There was a white cake, white "his and hers" towels, and a white runner. I wore a white dress with white flowers. It was my wedding, and I was standing at the altar, smiling and waiting for my groom. My groom wasn't there yet, but I knew he was coming. So, I continued to wait with a smile.

I used to work for Walmart as a cashier a while ago. It could be me actually getting married to a man on Earth, but I truly believe I represented the bride of Christ. It represented how we are waiting for Him with eagerness, to see the groom in all his splendor.

As I was watching Pastor Perry Stone, he talked about the Jewish feast days.

1. Passover (Leviticus 23:5) – Pointed to the Messiah as our Passover lamb (1 Corinthians 5:7) whose blood would be shed for our sins. Jesus was crucified during the time that the Passover was observed (Mark 14:12). Christ is a "lamb without blemish or defect" (1 Peter 1:19) because His life was completely free from sin (Hebrews 4:15). As

the first Passover marked the Hebrews' release from Egyptian slavery, so the death of Christ marks our release from the slavery of sin (Romans 8:2).

2. Unleavened Bread (Leviticus 23:6) – Pointed to the Messiah's sinless life (as leaven is a picture of sin in the Bible), making Him the perfect sacrifice for our sins. Jesus' body was in the grave during the first days of this feast, like a kernel of wheat planted and waiting to burst forth as the bread of life.

3. First Fruits (Leviticus 23:10) – Pointed to the Messiah's resurrection as the first fruits of the righteous. Jesus was resurrected on this very day, which is one of the reasons that Paul refers to him in 1 Corinthians 15:20 as the "first fruits from the dead."

4. Weeks or Pentecost (Leviticus 23:16) – Occurred fifty days after the beginning of the Feast of Unleavened Bread and pointed to the great harvest of souls and the gift of the Holy Spirit for both Jew and Gentile, who would be brought into the kingdom of God during the Church Age (see Acts 2). The Church was actually established on this day when God poured out His Holy Spirit and 3,000 Jews responded to Peter's great sermon and his first proclamation of the gospel.

5. Trumpets (Leviticus 23:24) – The first of the fall feasts. Many believe this day points to the Rapture of the Church when the Messiah Jesus will appear in the heavens as He

comes for His bride, the Church. The Rapture is always associated in Scripture with the blowing of a loud trumpet (1 Thessalonians 4:13-18 and 1 Corinthians 15:52).

6. Day of Atonement (Leviticus 23:27) – Many believe this prophetically points to the day of the Second Coming of Jesus when He will return to Earth. That will be the Day of Atonement for the Jewish remnant when they "look upon Him whom they have pierced," repent of their sins, and receive Him as their Messiah (Zechariah 12:10 and Romans 11:1-6, 25-36).

7. Tabernacles or Booths (Leviticus 23:34) – Many scholars believe that this feast day points to the Lord's promise that He will once again "tabernacle" with His people when He returns to reign over all the world (Micah 4:1-7).

Should Christians celebrate these Levitical feast days of Israel today? Whether or not a Christian celebrates the Jewish feast days would be a matter of conscience for the individual Christian. Colossians 2:16-17 tells us, "Therefore do not let anyone judge you by what you eat or drink, or with regard to a religious festival, a New Moon celebration or a Sabbath day. These are a shadow of the things that were to come; the reality, however, is found in Christ." Christians are not bound to observe the Jewish feasts the way an Old Testament Jew was, but we should not criticize another believer who does or does not observe these special days and feasts (Romans 14:5).

While it is not required for Christians to celebrate the Jewish feast days, it is beneficial to study them. Certainly, it could be beneficial to celebrate these days if it leads one to a greater understanding and appreciation for Christ's death and resurrection and the future promise of His coming. As Christians, if we choose to celebrate these special days, we should put Christ in the center of the celebration, as the One who came to fulfill the prophetic significance of each of them.

Also study the Harvest cycle, this will give you a greater understanding about the feast days and more on why the Jewish people celebrate these feasts.

The Banquet

June 2016

This is going to sound weird, but I was back in the medieval time era, and I remember seeing in the distance a crowd of people cheering and celebrating while walking toward the town hall where the banquet would be held. There were confetti and balloons, and the people who were coming to the banquet hall were very wealthy. Their vehicles and garments were a gold color, shiny and beautiful. I was shiny, as well. Now, the people from the town looked rundown and wore tattered clothes. Again, the banquet hall was a medieval style, but I know it's not going to look like that in heaven. It will be far more glorious.

As we entered the banquet hall, the doors shut behind us. There were two tall, large men guarding the doors to keep the outside crowd from coming in. I remember sitting down at the table and looking out the window at the people who were looking in on us. My heart cried for them, and I wanted to give them food to eat.

Then, all of a sudden, I was on outside looking in at the people sitting at the banquet table and wishing I could be a part of it. Hungry and thirsty, I banged on the windows for someone to let me inside to eat.

God gave me a perspective from both sides: one while sitting inside the banquet hall, and the other view as seen by the people who wished they could be a part of the banquet. By the end of the dream, I was sitting at the table eating and drinking along with everyone else, and we had a wonderful time at the banquet.

Will there be food in heaven? Will we need food to sustain us in heaven? Revelation 19:9 states, "Blessed are those who are invited to the marriage supper of the Lamb." People eat at a marriage supper, so it would be reasonable to expect a celebration involving food with the Lord. You are invited to the supper of the lamb. If you belong to Christ and live for Him, then you won't be one of those who are on the outside looking in.

Two principles emerge from Revelation 19:9 and similar passages. First, food will no longer be essential to sustain life in heaven. However, it seems people will eat together with the Lord in heaven. This is not to sustain life but rather to enjoy fellowship and to celebrate being together forever. Ultimately, eating together will be an act of giving glory to God, something commanded even for when we eat now: "So, whether you eat or drink, or whatever you do, do all to the glory of God" (1 Corinthians 10:31).

Matthew 8:11 discusses that many will come to eat at the future feast with the Lord: "I tell you, many will come from east and west, and recline at table with Abraham, Isaac, and Jacob in the kingdom of heaven." Here, it appears eating together with the Lord will take place even though food will not be required to sustain life. Luke 14:15 adds Jesus saying, "Blessed is everyone who will eat bread in the kingdom of

God!"

First, Jesus stated He would one day eat again with His followers: "Truly, I say to you, I will not drink again of the fruit of the vine until that day when I drink it new in the kingdom of God" (Mark 14:25). Second, the resurrected Jesus ate: "They gave him a piece of broiled fish, and he took it and ate before them" (Luke 24:42-43). Jesus also seems to have eaten in John 21:4-14.

It does not mean all people will eat in heaven, but at least it shows that Jesus ate after His resurrection.

The Parable of the Great Banquet
15When one of those at the table with him heard this, he said to Jesus, "Blessed is the one who will eat at the feast in the kingdom of God."

16Jesus replied: "A certain man was preparing a great banquet and invited many guests. 17At the time of the banquet he sent his servant to tell those who had been invited, 'Come, for everything is now ready.'

18"But they all alike began to make excuses. The first said, 'I have just bought a field, and I must go and see it. Please excuse me.'

19"Another said, 'I have just bought five yoke of oxen, and I'm on my way to try them out. Please excuse me.'

20"Still another said, 'I just got married, so I can't come.'

21"The servant came back and reported this to his master. Then the owner of the house became angry and ordered his servant, 'Go out quickly into the streets and alleys of the town and bring in the poor, the crippled, the blind and the lame.'

22'Sir,' the servant said, 'what you ordered has been done, but there is still room.'

²³ "Then the master told his servant, 'Go out to the roads and country lanes and compel them to come in, so that my house will be full. ²⁴I tell you, not one of those who were invited will get a taste of my banquet.'"

Luke 14:15-24 NIV

Out of the Darkness

My father was a person who had a hard time forgiving people. I had asked him about some things that happened when he was younger, and I could tell he never forgave that person for what they did to him. The situation is very personal, so I can't share it. My father held a lot of bitterness in his heart, and as the years went by, people did other things to him that he still didn't forgive.

One day, the Lord spoke to my heart and told me that He was going to take my dad because he refused to forgive others or ask God to help him with learning to forgive. I pleaded with God, "Please don't take him. Let me talk to him," and He allowed me.

I rushed to talk to my father, and when I told him what God told me, he started to cry. I told him what he must do: "Go and ask for forgiveness for not forgiving others." If he did that and truly meant it, God would allow him to live. My dad did it; he cried while asking God to forgive him.

After leaving my father, I went home and looked through my dream journal. I came across a dream about my mother, my father, and another person. All three were in a car, and my dad was in the backseat. They were driving over an icy lake, and as they were driving, the ice began to crack, and the car sunk into the lake. My mom and the other person got out of the car, but my dad was stuck inside. When I saw him sinking into the darkness of the water, I swam down, grabbed his hand, and pulled him up out of the darkness, saving him.

When I read that dream, I thought to myself, *Oh my gosh! It came true.* It was about five years prior. God was showing me that with His help, I was going to help pull my dad from the darkness of his heart. I cried and thanked God for giving me the courage and strength to tell my father that he needed to forgive.

God is big on forgiveness. We must forgive others for the wrong they do to us, or God won't forgive us for our wrongdoings to Him and others. It won't be easy, but it's necessary.

Has someone done something to you, and you refuse to forgive them? Have you done wrong to someone, and they haven't offered forgiveness?

When you ask for forgiveness, you're taking that power back, even if they don't forgive you. If you ask for forgiveness from the person you hurt and they won't forgive, you will have done your part. Their refusal to forgive will be between them and God.

The Bible gives us the costly requirement for God's forgiveness: "Without the shedding of blood, there is no forgiveness" (Hebrews 9:22). In the Old Testament, the continual sacrifices of unblemished lambs were required to satisfy God's wrath and judgment. However, Jesus Christ, the Son of God, died on a Roman cross and became the ultimate, once-and-for-all sacrifice for our sins. Jesus purchased God's forgiveness on our behalf when He became the Lamb of God and died on the cross for you and me.

For Christ died for sins once for all, the righteous for the unrighteous, to bring you to God.

1 Peter 3:18 NIV

In him we have redemption through his blood, the forgiveness of sins, in accordance with the riches of God's grace.

Ephesians 1:7 NIV

A believer receives God's forgiveness when he repents of sin and places his faith in Jesus Christ for salvation; all of his sins are forgiven forever. That includes past, present, and future, big or small. Jesus died to pay the penalty for all of our sins, and once they are forgiven, they are all forgiven (Colossians 1:14; Acts 10:43). However, when we stumble, we are called to confess our sins: "If we confess our sins, he is faithful and just and will forgive us our sins and purify us from all unrighteousness" (1 John 1:9).

Yes, Christians do sin (1 John 1:8), but the Christian life is not to be identified by a life of sin. Believers are a new creation (2 Corinthians 5:17). We have the Holy Spirit in us producing good fruit (Galatians 5:22-23). A Christian life should be a changed life. A person who claims to be a believer yet continually lives a life that says otherwise should question the genuineness of his faith. No matter how many times they sin, Christians are forgiven as long as they truly repent and ask God for help. At the same time, Christians should live a progressively more holy life as they grow closer to Christ.

Hadassah Cohen

The Unforgiving Servant

[21] *Then Peter came up and said to him, "Lord, how often will my brother sin against me, and I forgive him? As many as seven times?"* [22] *Jesus said to him, "I do not say to you seven times, but seventy-seven times.*

[23] *"Therefore the kingdom of heaven may be compared to a king who wished to settle accounts with his servants.* [24] *When he began to settle, one was brought to him who owed him ten thousand talents.* [25] *And since he could not pay, his master ordered him to be sold, with his wife and children and all that he had, and payment to be made.* [26] *So the servant fell on his knees, imploring him, 'Have patience with me, and I will pay you everything.'* [27] *And out of pity for him, the master of that servant released him and forgave him the debt.* [28] *But when that same servant went out, he found one of his fellow servants who owed him a hundred denarii, and seizing him, he began to choke him, saying, 'Pay what you owe.'* [29] *So his fellow servant fell down and pleaded with him, 'Have patience with me, and I will pay you.'* [30] *He refused and went and put him in prison until he should pay the debt.* [31] *When his fellow servants saw what had taken place, they were greatly distressed, and they went and reported to their master all that had taken place.* [32] *Then his master summoned him and said to him, 'You wicked servant! I forgave you all that debt because you pleaded with me.* [33] *And should not you have had mercy on your fellow servant, as I had mercy on you?'* [34] *And in anger his master delivered him to the jailers, until he should pay all his debt.* [35] *So also my heavenly Father will do to every one of you, if you do not forgive your brother from your heart."*

Matthew 18:21-35 ESV

Inca Indian

September 2017

I was in a beautiful garden, and there was a lake. A man was kneeling beside the lake. He was an Inca Indian. While kneeling near the water, he held out his hand that had food in it and waited for something to come out of the lake.

As I looked on, I saw a great leopard with four wings come out of the water and eat the food from out of the man's hand. But, as I looked on, I heard, "September." I knew in my spirit that it had something to do with our food. Then, I remembered the dream of me working at Walmart and getting married in September.

After the beast finished eating the food out of the Indian's hand, the creature, who had muscles like a man, rose on his back legs and beat up the Inca Indian. I'm still waiting for God to show me what this dream means.

I believe this dream and the dream of the bride are part of the same dream because both had the month of September.

Massive Tsunami

March 2016

My family and I were in a house. All of a sudden, I saw a massive wave, which almost touched the sky, coming unto the land. I was on top of the wave looking down. I'm not sure why I was on top of the wave, but I believe I was raptured. At that moment, I was able to see between the house and the wave. Then, the dream switched to me sitting in the bed of a truck. I believe I was traveling through a southern state to a new destination. I'm not sure how I knew it was a southern state, but somehow, it felt like it in the dream. The dream stopped as we were traveling down the road.

I'm not sure of the meaning of this dream. It could be to warn of an actual tsunami, or the events that are coming will be so massive that it will move us from our original location.

The Lord will reveal what he needs us to do. Be prayerful; ask God.

Streams of Missiles

June 2016

My father called me at 3:30 a.m. and said, "I had a dream." He told me that his heart was beating fast, and he was shaking all over. I asked him what happened in the dream. Keep in mind that my dad doesn't dream as I do. When he has a dream, it's a prophetic one.

He said he was living in the senior apartment complex where he was currently living, and then it started getting dark outside. Someone said, "The sky looks weird." They agreed to hold hands just in case something happened.

When they all looked up at the sky, they saw streams of missiles coming from every direction: north, south, east, and west. They were going into the air.

My father told me that he said to himself, *When that hits, it will be an enormous explosion. The sound will be so great, even the dead will hear it.*

While he was saying it, the missiles collided with each other, causing a bright light to illuminate the sky across the world. Then parts of the world began to fall away like puzzle pieces. Where there were skies and lights, it became darkness. There was no longer any light, skies, land, or seas. Absolutely nothing.

They were in total darkness, but he still felt himself holding hands with someone. He could also talk to the ones around him.

"What happened?" he asked the others.

"My eyes began to melt in my sockets," one person told him.

Some others said their skin fell off their bones because of the heat.

And this shall be the plague wherewith the LORD will smite all the people that have fought against Jerusalem; Their flesh shall consume away while they stand upon their feet, and their eyes shall consume away in their holes, and their tongue shall consume away in their mouth.

Zechariah 14:12 KJV

[11] And I saw a great white throne, and him that sat on it, from whose face the earth and the heaven fled away; and there was found no place for them.

[12] And I saw the dead, small and great, stand before God; and the books were opened: and another book was opened, which is the book of life: and the dead were judged out of those things which were written in the books, according to their works.

[13] And the sea gave up the dead which was in it; death and hell delivered up the dead which was in them: and they were judged every man according to their works.

[14] And death and hell were cast into the lake of fire. This is the second death.

[15] And whosoever was not found written in the book of life was cast into the lake of fire."

Revelation 20:11-15 KJV

It's amazing how God, the Lord Jesus Christ, shows us things that will happen in the future.

Surely the Sovereign LORD does nothing without revealing his plan to his servants the prophets.

Amos 3:7 NIV

The Change

July 2016

One day, my son was playing his video game. I was laying on the couch and fell asleep. I had a dream I was outside talking to a man who seemed to have feelings for me. While I was talking to him, there were many people around us talking and enjoying festivities. Suddenly, I felt a change in my body. It happened quickly.

In a moment, in the twinkling of an eye, at the last trumpet. For the trumpet will sound, and the dead will be raised imperishable, and we shall be changed.
                                1 Corinthians 15:52 KJV (Blue Letter Bible)

In an instant, I began floating up into the air. I knew what was going on, and I was so happy. Then I started to see many more people going up. We were all going up at the same time. As I was going up, I looked down at the guy who liked me and told him bye. Stunned, he looked around while wondering what was going on. Then, I woke up. When I woke up, my eyes were big. I looked around at my surroundings, wondering if I was in the sky.

My son looked at me and said, "Momma, you were talking

in your sleep. I couldn't make out what you were saying, though."

I was so mad that I started kicking my legs like a child having a tantrum. It felt so real. I thought it actually happened.

I praised Jesus Christ for allowing me to see that glorious day, for one day, it will be a reality. For this perishable body must put on the imperishable, and this mortal body must put on immortality. When the perishable puts on the imperishable, and the mortal puts on immortality, then shall come to pass the saying that is written:

"Death is swallowed up in victory."
"O death, where is your victory?
O death, where is your sting?"

1 Corinthians 15:54-55 ESV

He will wipe away every tear from their eyes, and death shall be no more, neither shall there be mourning, nor crying, nor pain anymore, for the former things have passed away.

Revelation 21:4 ESV

Have you ever had a rapture dream? Did it feel real?

The Painting

July 2017

I was riding in a fire truck with a friend of mine who was a fireman. He was called to the house of a little old woman whose upstairs was on fire. He went in to try and save the lady. He said he felt drawn to a painting that was in the old woman's room. As he held the picture, he began hearing voices and knew in his spirit that there was something wrong. After putting out the fire, he rushed the painting to the fire truck.

"There's a demon in this painting," the fireman said.

We began to pray and plead the blood of Jesus, asking God to protect us from evil. My friend placed a black tarp over the painting, using it as a barrier to keep the demon in the picture. He believed the demon was the one who started the fire to kill the little old woman, and he knew he had to keep it safe. So, he put the painting in the truck and took it to the fire station.

The next day when my friend went to his truck, the painting was gone. He searched around the fire station for it and found it hanging on the wall. He came and told me what had happened.

"I hear voices in the station," he said, then quickly placed the black tarp over the painting again and removed it.

Suddenly, the dream changed. I was a security guard at an

art museum. As I walked around looking at the beautiful paintings, I noticed the demonic painting. "OH, NO!" I said to myself.

Then something strange began to happen. The security guards were paralyzed and in a trance. Someone wheeled them out on a dolly, one by one, until it was just me and a few others. I had a vision in the dream that the demon was going to start a fire to try and kill me.

Shortly after the vision, the fire alarm went off. We tried to get everyone out, but the doors were programmed to shut and lock automatically when the alarm sounded. My son was in the museum at the time, also. I shouted for him to run. There was a large, heavy door that was closing and would have trapped my son inside. I ran and put my arm in the door to hold it open, but a supernatural force was pushing it closed. I yelled to God and asked him to give me the strength to open the door. The Lord gave me supernatural strength, and my son was able to escape. While I held the door, there was a force trying to shut it again. So, I called on Jesus, and I received more supernhuman strength to continue holding the door open, but only for a moment. Then, the door shut, and I was locked inside the museum. So, I ran up the stairs to the roof. The fire had started. I was trapped, and I died.

When I opened my eyes, I was hovering in hell. The demon grabbed my arm and tried to claim my soul. However, the angel of the Lord was there right beside me, and with his teeth clenched together in anger, he bellowed, "NO! SHE BELONGS TO ME!"

As the demon let go of my arm, the angel of the Lord told me, "Come on, Augustine. Let's go."

I felt like a little kid who just got saved from a bully. I looked up at the angel with my eyes like the animated character in the movie *Puss in Boots*, the black part making up most of my eyes and only a little white showing. I was extremely grateful to the angel of the Lord.

As we were floating upward, a bright light surrounded us. I didn't want to look down, but I did. When I looked down, I saw a lake of lava and millions of souls crying and calling out to God. My heart sank. I cried hard in the dream for those souls.

"Keep looking up! Keep looking up!" said the angel.

When I woke up, I was still crying for the lost souls I had seen in my dream.

The Light in the Earth

August 19, 2017

There was a disturbance in the earth. I'm not sure what kind of disturbance, but I sensed it in my spirit in the dreams. There was a female angel that came down in a chariot with horses and who had the glory of God surrounding her. But, when I saw her, she was in human form. I was the only one who could see her true form and not have to shield my eyes. When the angel came down, she passed through the gates where witches were and went into the earth. The angel took a precious artifact that the witches were holding that belonged to heaven.

I watched as the angel went into the earth. She went far into the ground, and as she was coming up, I saw a big ball of light. Once she hit the surface, she shot straight up into the heavens. She moved fast. It was quicker than any propulsion we have here on earth. Then she came back down to help us fight evil in her human form. I looked to the sky, feeling like something like a major disaster was getting ready to happen.

In my dream, I heard a voice say, "All the closed down Marsh stores will become FEMA camps." I don't know if the message was from God. Only time will tell.

I believe the big ball of light the angel removed from the earth was dead in Christ.

A New Thing in Us!

August 2017

In this dream, I had on a white robe and was standing in the pulpit, speaking to a black church. An African woman approached me and asked, "Why should I believe in a God that will send me to hell?"

"God doesn't send anybody to hell," I told her. "We send ourselves."

While I talked with her, the spirit of the Lord began to open her heart. How did I know? Because God made it to where I was able to see through her eyes to her heart, and I saw her heart open. She gave her life to Christ. The Holy Spirit fell on us, and as the Lord spoke to her through me, she began asking more questions that I don't recall.

The power of God was so strong in the dream that God gave me the words to say to her. Alone, without God, I didn't know what to say.

As I sat down in a chair in front of the choir stand, the pastor came over and placed his elbow on the arm of my chair. While bent over looking at me, he put his foot on the bottom of my chair and started shaking it in disrespect.

"Could you not shake my chair?" I said through gritted teeth.

He stopped shaking my chair and went back to his seat.

That's when I stood up and said, "It's amazing how much the church is divided." My comment was certainly not meant in a good way.

Then the Holy Spirit fell on me and said, "God is getting ready to do a new thing! God is going to bring in men, women, and children. He is tired of the division in the black churches."

God uses people to speak to those who need him.

See, I am doing a new thing! Now it springs up; do you not perceive it?

Isaiah 43:19 NIV

In the last days, God says, I will pour out my Spirit on all people. Your sons and daughters will prophesy, your young men will see visions, your old men will dream dreams.

Acts 2:17

Fake Christians

September 23, 2017

I was left behind to see a glimpse of the seven-year tribulation period. Christians and non-Christians were suffering great distress during the tribulation period. Fake Christians hunted a real Christian woman, and there were all kinds of imposters. They knew the language and the body language of Christians, but they weren't true believers in the church—just like today, but worse.

The government offered those in need of everyday necessities a bribe to hunt down all Christians. In return, they would get food and fame, but it was only for those who didn't take the mark of the beast. The government knew the Christians wouldn't take the mark, so they needed people to spy and act like them to trick them and find out where they were hiding. They would hurt anybody who tried to stop them from getting money and fame.

Revelation 16 gives a brief glimpse of just how awful it will be for the residents of the earth at that time:

[18] And there were voices, and thunders, and lightnings; and there was a great earthquake, such as was not since men were upon the earth, so mighty an earthquake, and *so great. [19] And*

the great city was divided into three parts, and the cities of the nations fell: and great Babylon came in remembrance before God, to give unto her the cup of the wine of the fierceness of his wrath. [20]And every island fled away, and the mountains were not found. [21]And there fell upon men a great hail out of heaven, every stone about the weight of a talent (100 lbs.): and men blasphemed God because of the plague of the hail; for the plague thereof was exceeding great.
Revelation 16:18-21 KJV (Blue Letter Bible)

And the fifth angel blew his trumpet, and I saw a star fallen from heaven to earth, and he was given the key to the shaft of the bottomless pit. [2]He opened the shaft of the bottomless pit, and from the shaft rose smoke like the smoke of a great furnace, and the sun and the air were darkened with the smoke from the shaft. [3]Then from the smoke came locusts on the earth, and they were given power like the power of scorpions of the earth. [4]They were told not to harm the grass of the earth or any green plant or any tree, but only those people who do not have the seal of God on their foreheads. [5]They were allowed to torment them for five months, but not to kill them, and their torment was like the torment of a scorpion when it stings someone. [6]And in those days people will seek death and will not find it. They will long to die, but death will flee from them.
Revelation 9:1-6 ESV

The Chip

I was in a fish market, speaking to people about Jesus Christ, and a song came on the radio. *People get ready! Jesus is coming. Soon we'll be going home.*

"Do you believe in Jesus?" I asked the lady at the counter.

Without saying a word, she got up and turned the radio to something else.

The dream changed; I was a man. Looking through his eyes, I was in a heavily-guarded factory, and the guards were tracking everyone. I wanted to go out, but they had to scan a chip to make sure it was me. I didn't know I had a chip in my body. I had gone to the doctor for surgery for something else, not for a microchip. They had implanted a chip in me without me knowing.

Here, I think I was looking through the eyes of a humanoid, as well. When he went to get back online, they did surgery and put him back like he was before. I was trying to fight them off. Then they opened up a cave-like door that led to the chaos-filled streets. It was so bad that when I got to a street corner, I could see body bags and bodies piled up. I was horrified.

The Lord shows his people things that will soon take place so people can make a choice either to accept Christ or to stay in the world. This is not about fear, but to a certain degree, it is a Godly fear because while you don't want to face what is soon to come, you don't want to go to hell either. God loves you so much. He wouldn't be trying to get your attention through other people's dreams and visions if He didn't. He loves you that much.

Ice Age

April 1, 2018 – Easter

My sister and I were on Earth, but the galaxy was messing up. Somehow, the universe and a lot of other nebulas were flying by us. They were so close that we were able to jump into them. We fell through the atmosphere and into the ocean. Some items from Earth were in the ocean, and when we got out of the ocean, we fell on the land like the ocean was upside down. Crazy, I know.

I saw a map of the United States. Thick ice covered half of the northern hemisphere; it was a new Ice Age. The bottom part was warm, almost like in the movie *The Day After Tomorrow*, where half of America was covered in ice. It was so weird. Many different things started happening on Earth. I don't know if this is going to happen, but this is what I saw.

Dad's Dream

Winter 2017

My dad said he dreamed that he was walking down the street to the store, and an out-of-control car was coming toward him. He jumped behind a tree, and the vehicle crashed into the tree. He said he went over to see if the person was okay, but there was no driver, only a passenger. All of a sudden, he heard the most horrifying sound of cars and trucks crashing all at once. No one was in the cars or trucks. Families had vanished, and planes fell from the sky because no pilots were flying the aircrafts.

He woke up terrified and praying he would not see in real life what he had seen in his dream.

[40]*Then shall two be in the field; the one shall be taken, and the other left.*

[41]*Two women shall be grinding at the mill; the one shall be taken, and the other left.*

[42]*Watch therefore: for ye know not what hour your Lord doth come.*

[43]*But know this, that if the goodman of the house had known in what watch the thief would come, he would have watched, and would not have suffered his house to be broken up.*

[44]Therefore be ye also ready: for in such an hour as ye think not the Son of man cometh.

[45]Who then is a faithful and wise servant, whom his lord hath made ruler over his household, to give them meat in due season?

[46]Blessed is that servant, whom his lord when he cometh shall find so doing.

[47]Verily I say unto you, That he shall make him ruler over all his goods.

[48]But and if that evil servant shall say in his heart, My lord delayeth his coming;

[49]And shall begin to smite his fellow servants and to eat and drink with the drunken;

[50]The lord of that servant shall come in a day when he looketh not for him, and in an hour that he is not aware of,

[51]And shall cut him asunder, and appoint him his portion with the hypocrites: there shall be weeping and gnashing of teeth.

Matthew 24:40-51 KJV

The Lady of Chaos

December 4, 2018

I was at work doing my job as an assembler. I was pressing the bearings into my parts when from over my right shoulder, I saw a woman looking at me. Her hand was on my shoulder. I thought it was one of the women in the area, so I thought nothing of it. I thought she had gone past me, but when I looked to my left to see who it was, there was not a woman in my area at that time. My co-worker, Terry, who's a man, saw me standing there with big eyes.

The first thing out of his mouth was, "She was on you."

"WHAT!?" I said.

"She was on you," he told me.

"You saw her?" I asked.

He replied, "Yes. She was behind you like when a person comes up close to your back to surprise you. It was like that."

"WHAT!?" I told him. "I only saw half of her face because she looked around my glasses and said something in my ear. It was a female's voice. I don't know what she said, though. I couldn't make it out."

Terry said, "The woman is in her late 30's, early 40's."

"YES," I said, dumbfounded that he knew this information.

He saw her, too, but he had more information on her than I

did. She was a thin white woman with dusty-brown hair and silver-blue eyes. I pleaded the blood of Jesus.

Terry and I don't know what to make of it or why we saw her. It didn't feel like I knew her, but maybe she knew me.

My other co-worker, who was a Korean woman, started treating me weirdly. She had never been upset with me until after that encounter. The other women in that area started on me, as well. Now I know it was the spirit of confusion, and the reason why I was removed from that area was because of the women. They started the trouble, lying about me for no reason.

As for the women who started all the chaos, two are no longer around. They were fired, and the Korean woman changed to another shift.

I'm not sure what to make of this situation. That was a day of confusion, and everyone will have days like it.

For God is not the author of confusion, but of peace, as in all churches of the saints.

1 Corinthians 14:33 KJV

Single Men and Women

I met my son's father at the age of twenty. We started as friends. I knew him for four years and stayed a virgin until I was 23-½ years old. People don't believe me when I tell them. I guess it's because meeting someone who has kept their virginity until that age is a rarity, especially in the days we live in now. People who are virgins are teased, but I think it's beautiful. It tells a lot about the person for them to decide to wait for that special person before having sex.

At the time, my son's father had a four-year-old daughter, and that little girl stole my heart. She was so sweet and kind. She had a wonderful father who worked two to three jobs to make ends meet. I applaud him for that. In today's world, you don't find too many fathers doing that. We ended up getting married but divorced five years later. We are still friends; however, he has moved on with his life, and I moved on with mine. That was my first marriage and his second.

Three years passed, and I hadn't gone on any dates. I didn't want any man. My focus was on expanding my education. So, I went to college and graduated with an Associate's degree in Auto and Diesel Technology and Diesel Management. I was proud of myself, a single mom raising a child. It was not easy, but it was worth it. By the time I reached my mid-40s, I had decided it was time I started dating and ventured out into the online dating scene where I met a few men. Being 240-pounds and only standing 5'1", I had very low self-esteem. So, when a man started asking me questions, commenting about my body, or making vulgar statements, it was enough to upset me to the point where I stopped online dating for six months. But, when I found myself getting lonely again, I went to a different dating site—a Christian website. I thought for sure I would find someone who loves God and would respect me as a woman. Nope! That site was just as bad as the first one. No one wanted to talk about our Father God. They only talked about the sex god.

So, I started playing their game, and when I played their game, I got noticed by men. That led to me becoming something I never thought I would be—promiscuous. I believed if I gave myself away, I would find a boyfriend. WRONG! My promiscuous nature only resulted in me feeling worthless, unloved, and ugly. That's not who I was; I was living a lie.

I cried out to God, asking Him to help me, but despite stopping "being easy" for six months, I would start again. I was a hypocrite until one day God spoke to my heart, and with gnashed teeth, He said, "STOP CASTING YOUR PEARLS BEFORE SWINE."

That day, I dropped to the floor in shame. I felt pure agony knowing I had hurt my God's heart.

Crying uncontrollably, I asked Him, "Then why are You keeping me single this long if You don't want me to date?" Then I realized it wasn't that He didn't want me to date. The problem was the type of men that I was dating.

After that, I stopped for about a year, but once again, I

started back to my sinful way. This time, I dated two men at the same time. My spirit began to convince me that if I didn't stop, God would make it where I wouldn't have a choice, and my punishment could last for a lifetime.

I asked for forgiveness and pleaded with God to help me to be a better person and to remove the desires until He sends me that person who he wants me to be with. I know now who I am. I'm a child of God, and He loves me. I don't need any man to define me. I have the best man in my life that loves me and treats me with respect, and that's my God. He is everything to me and more. I could never repay Him for saving and protecting me. He knows me better than I know myself.

God knows we will fall sometimes, but don't you stay down. Get up, dust yourself off, and keep following Christ. The thing that separates us from the world is that the world can't handle the pressure, but as Christians, we put our faith in Christ. He will help us through everything if we trust Him. Some Christians lose their faith in Christ and think they can handle the situation themselves. Don't make that mistake. Keep believing and trusting in Christ. He will show up and show out in your life. Just give Him a chance.

If you are single, be patient. When it's time, God will show you who your mate will be. Use this time of singleness to learn more about God and grow closer to Him. I'm not saying you're not going to have sexual desires. It's natural, but trust that your every need will be fulfilled in His time, and it will be well worth the wait once you are blessed with the mate who He has for you.

We, as Christians, can't live like the world and expect our witness to be effective. I will pray for all my single sisters and brothers. I know this life is not easy, and fighting sexual temptation can be hard. I once felt like you, but I had to put my flesh under subjection. I refused to let it rule me. I would rule it through prayer and fasting.

"These things I have spoken to you, that in Me you may have peace. In the world you will have tribulation; but be of good cheer, I have overcome the world."

John 16:33 NKJV

"For I know the plans I have for you," declares the Lord, "plans to prosper you and not to harm you, plans to give you hope and a future."

Jeremiah 29:11 NIV

Get Your Ticket

December 17, 2019

<u>Rapture Dream Parable</u>
My son, my sister, and I went to the mall to ride on the riverboat. After we paid for our tickets, I left them in the mall and returned to the car. When my son came back to the car, he told me that we needed to leave to make it to the boat by 4:15 p.m.

"Here I come," I replied while gathering my stuff.

As we started walking towards the boat, I realized I had left my ticket in my other bag. I told my son to go ahead, and I would catch up. I ran back to the car to get my bag, and my son and my sister were running ahead.

"Wait for me," I called out, but they had run so far ahead of me that I couldn't see them anymore. *Where did they go?* I thought to myself.

Saddened that they didn't wait, I walked back to the car. As I returned to the car, I saw a model of the boat on the river. The people were happy, cheering, and celebrating as they boarded the boat, but they looked like ants on the model. I heard my son's voice clearly; he was happy and cheering, as well.

"Don't leave me! Don't leave me," I screamed while thinking to myself, *Oh no! I'm going to face the horrors that are in the book of Revelation.*

I woke up crying, repenting, and praying that I would be worthy to be taken in the RAPTURE. I was so busy helping everyone to prepare and making sure they had their ticket that I left my ticket. I was distracted when I should have kept my ticket close to me. The ticket represented Jesus, and the boat was heaven.

I'm not saying the rapture will happen at 4:15 p.m. That was just the time in my dream that the boat was to arrive. Per the Bible, no one knows the day or hour. Sometimes the Lord allows the person to be left behind in dreams so they can tell others to be prepared for the departure.

I looked up what 415 means in Hebrew on graceintorah.net, and this is what I learned.

4 = DALETH – numerical value of four.
Pictographic meaning door, draw out or in, knock, path, way, portal to heaven, dominion, control, bough, and branch.

1 = ALEPH – numerical value of one.
Pictographic meaning strength, ox, chief, prince, leader, first.

5 = HEY – numerical value of five.
Pictographic meaning breath, air, spirit, and behold (to make known).

WHAT! Only God can do things like this, I cried. God gave me a rapture dream, and the numbers represent his son Jesus

Christen – *Door, Chief, Prince, Leader, The First, Air, Spirit.*

I hope this dream will help make others realize that Jesus is speaking to His people to lead others to Christ so they won't be left behind.

Accept Christ in your heart today. Repent of your sins, and ask Him to come into your heart and live with you forever. Amen.

After the Rapture

February 22, 2020

I believe it was an after-rapture dream. In the dream, I was in my house staring out of the window. When all of a sudden, the buildings looked like they were being stretched repeatedly. It almost looked like when you blow up a long-shaped balloon and then when the air is released, it goes back to its original shape. It was weird, I know. The people on the sideline were pale-faced demons who looked like regular men. They were waiting for the word to be given to attack.

They were sitting like people waiting for the show to start. That is the way this group of men was sitting and watching us. There was a head demon angel watching the people go about their day. He paced back and forth like he couldn't wait to get to the people. There was an evacuation happening, and people took whatever transportation possible—car, bike, motorcycle. Traffic was backed up for miles.

I had gone back to a neighborhood to make sure everyone was out. This woman, who had a nice home, didn't want to leave. Her sister and her boyfriend were at her house. I told them several times that we needed to leave. I started packing up some things of hers, and when I turned around, she was outside talking to the head demon and hugging him. He was touching her butt like they had known each other for years. I was dumbfounded.

She came back inside the house and told us that the man said we didn't have to leave. I told her that she could stay, and then I ran out of that house so fast and down the street to get away. When I looked back, the head demon was watching me run away. Then, I saw the sister running behind me. She was far off but moving like the superhero Flash; she was moving faster than me. I thought to myself, *How stupid is that woman to hold on to her house.*

Chaos makes people do some strange things; all common sense goes out the window. But this dream was almost like when Lot's wife looked back and perished, just like the woman in the dream. Those demons were going to harm her, and she couldn't see it. She loved the things in this world so much that she was willing to die to hold on to them.

What are you holding on to that is keeping you from committing your life to Jesus? Is it money, sex, fame? These are the things Satan uses to trap mankind.

Give your life to Christ, and you will have the best that is yet to come. See you in the air, my friend, and keep looking up. WE ARE ALMOST HOME!

POEMS

A PLACE

Written in 2019

My beautiful child
One day you will know what I mean
When I say I love you!

The sparkle in your eyes when I am nigh
Fills my heart with joy it's true
Like a husband comes to take his wife,
You are my life.
That's the reason why I died for you
So we can be together.

I prepared a place for us
No corruption will be among us
There will be peace, joy, abundance of love
My father will sing before us.

Hold your head up
Live for me
Will meet you in the clouds
Their rewards will be.

Hadassah Cohen

SEARCHING

Written in 1993

As the rain falls, the grass grows
Lord, you've been good to me
How could no one ever know?

Trials and tests come my way
My heart is laden down, that I can say
The past haunts me
My mind goes back
How could I have ever made it without a track of footprints.

Though my mind clashes
My spirits are down
My past is thrown in the sea, to never again be found.

Now I can say, "THANK YOU, LORD!"
For being there for me when I needed you the most
Riding in my caddy, I glance to the sky; "Hi, Daddy."
Tears fill my eyes as your embrace makes me sigh
"I LOVE YOU, LORD!" comes out of my mouth
Response in my ears says, "Come to my house."

As I fall asleep, I begin to weep
Saying, "What's going on?"
A gentle voice chimed
My face began to shine.
Looking up and seeing a man – a man so bright

"You are My Light."
"Show the people who I AM and what I can do;
Let them know I AM real. I LOVE YOU, MY CHILD!
You are mine forever!
I will never let you go; that you do know!

I will see you soon
Don't let no one turn you around
I am coming quickly
So you will need not wear a frown."

A Virgin

A virgin is pure
A virgin shines bright
A virgin knows when the time is right

Keep your virginity as long as you are alive
Don't give it to anyone who tells you a lie
They tell you, "If you love me, you will do it."
You say, "I'm not going to do it, not even for you."

Stand up, my people, no matter who you are
Don't let no one talk you into it and leave a scar
Stand straight and stand tall, those of you who were invaded
Don't blame yourself for what happened; God will repay
Over time the wounds will heal
But don't let bitterness overpower you and cause you to steal

Keep looking up towards heaven
Keep your eyes on the prize
One day soon, we will rise
And the pain and bitterness will be no more
We will be in God's house forevermore.

I was fifteen years old when I wrote the poem, *A Virgin*. I stayed a virgin until I was 23-½ years old and got married. My friends use to tease and laugh at me because I didn't want to give it up easy like they did just because a guy commented about how I was pretty or cute. I knew who I was and didn't need a man to validate me. I was a beautiful woman who wanted to remain pure until the Lord blessed me with that right person.

Sure, it was hard seeing my sisters and female friends having fun with their boyfriends, but I was determined not to give in. And yes, I could have still had a boyfriend, but then chances are I would have had to deal with the temptation from him to be sexually intimate. At one point, I had a boyfriend, but after I expressed wanted to be married before having sex, he wasn't in agreement to wait. So, I let him go. I was determined not to let society brainwash me into letting go of something so sacred to me. I wrote the poem, *A Virgin*, to encourage other men and women to hold on to their virginity. There is nothing wrong with remaining a virgin until that special and deserving person comes along. It was worth it for me.

Note from the Author

I wouldn't change a thing in my life. I want to see what God has to show me now and in the future.

I love all races and cultures, and I don't hate anyone. God loves everyone, but He will not love sin. We have to choose to change our lives and allow Christ to change our hearts and keep our tongue through the Holy Spirit.

^{9}That if thou shalt confess with thy mouth the Lord Jesus, and shalt believe in thine heart that God hath raised him from the dead, thou shalt be saved. ^{10}For with the heart, man believeth unto righteousness; and with the mouth confession is made unto salvation.

Romans 10:9-10 KJV

It has been a pleasure writing this book. Please check out my online store at Insaneg2.com. God Bless you, and thank you for purchasing my book.

Made in the USA
Monee, IL
02 September 2020